POSITIVE P

# Help your child through

# SECONDARY SCHOOL

PETER DOWNES & CAREY BENNET

## Hodder & Stoughton

A MEMBER OF THE HODDER HEADLINE GROUP

A catalogue record for this title is available from The British Library

ISBN 0 340 697490

First published 1997
Impression number 10  9  8  7  6  5  4  3  2  1
Year                    2002  2001  2000  1999  1998  1997

Typeset by Wearset, Boldon, Tyne and Wear.
Printed in Great Britain for Hodder & Stoughton Educational, a division of Hodder
Headline Plc, 338 Euston Road, London NW1 3BH by Cox and Wyman Ltd,
Reading, Berks.

# Contents

# About the authors

**Peter Downes** has taught languages in independent and state schools and has been a comprehensive school Head for over twenty years. As a former President of the Secondary Heads Association, he has wide experience of the secondary sector in this country. He is committed to the development of parental involvement in secondary education and is an active supporter of Parent Teacher Associations. He is now a freelance educational consultant with a special interest in financial management, educational publishing and school improvement through Governor and parent involvement in schools. He has two sons who have successfully survived being educated in their father's school.

**Carey Bennet** is an Education Officer with Cambridgeshire Local Education Authority, providing advice and support to headteachers, Governors and parents. Having trained as an Art teacher, she did doctoral research at Oxford University and taught in secondary schools before working with Leicestershire and then Cambridgeshire LEAs. Her particular interest is the development of partnership between parents and schools. She has two sons for whom secondary education is an adventure to look forward to.

# Acknowledgements

We would like to thank all those who have helped us in the writing of this book. Much of the inspiration has come from visiting schools in this country and in the USA, Canada, Australia and New Zealand and from talking with teachers, Governors, LEA officers, parents and pupils over many years – too many to mention by name.

We would like to thank the Education Group of the Hinchingbrooke School Association from whose discussions the idea of writing this book first arose and particularly Martin Patterson and Sue Shorter.

Our thanks to all those who have supplied information or read and commented on various sections of the book in draft: Richard Haycraft, Brian Gale, Ruth Diffey, Dave Castell, Duncan Grey, Pauline Maskell, Paul Wright, Richard Harrison, Peter Cunningham and Pamela Downes. The help of the Kirklees Education Advisory Service is gratefully acknowledged in connection with one of the appendices.

Although we have drawn on our experience with the Secondary Heads Association and the Cambridgeshire Local Education Authority, we write here in a personal capacity.

## *An important note*

This book is written in terms of the education system in England and Wales. In Scotland and Northern Ireland there are different arrangements and you would need to check on points of detail (see the relevant addresses in Appendix 12). The general advice will be relevant to all readers.

Some points of detail may be affected by local or national political decisions.

# Introduction

The last few years have seen many changes in the education system in this country. Scarcely a day passes without some new development or some frightening story being reported in the press. Parents with children approaching secondary school could well be forgiven for feeling bewildered and even anxious about what lies ahead for their children.

*Help your Child through Secondary School* has been written to:

- provide clear information about how secondary education is organised
- inform you of your rights and responsibilities in relation to your children's education
- give guidance on how you can help your sons and daughters achieve their best and be happy at school
- enable you to become effective supporters of your child's school and thus contribute to the important task of raising educational standards.

We do not claim to lay out a blueprint for success. No such blueprint is available because every child is different and schools vary considerably in the way they are organised, even though they are all engaged in essentially the same process. There is no single model for an ideal school but good schools will have a combination of the features mentioned in this book. Remember that changes are always taking place and it is essential that, having read this book as a general introduction, you check out points of detail in the particular school your children attend.

What is clear is that children achieve well at school when their parents take an interest in what they are doing and have a positive attitude towards the school. It is not uncommon for parents who have taken a close interest in their child's work at primary school to lessen their involvement as he or she gets older. However, the evidence suggests that a child's need for support and encouragement does not end at the moment of transfer from primary to secondary school.

This book is rooted in the belief that you as parents can make a big difference to your child's progress. Children spend 85 per cent of their waking hours outside school so your role is crucial to long-term success. We hope that our advice will go some way towards helping you in this important task.

# *How to use this book*

Although we have tried to lay out the contents in a reasonably logical order, this is not the kind of book you will necessarily want to read through from beginning to end. Study the contents list carefully first. If your child is already in a secondary school, you will want to skip straight over Chapter 1, for example. Some of the chapters on problems and difficulties may not affect you at all.

Where there are more detailed explanations of technical issues, you will find these in the appendices at the end of the book. In many cases, you may want to find out more about a particular topic so there are references to other books and we have given the names and addresses of organisations which can give you further help. There is also an appendix explaining the abbreviations which are most frequently used in talking about education today.

For the sake of simplicity, we have used the word 'parent' throughout the text although we recognise that the person responsible for looking after a child may be a step-parent, a foster-parent, a grand-parent or another person acting as carer. In referring to the child, rather than keep repeating 'he or she', 'his or her', we have simply used either the masculine or the feminine form. Other than in the section where we are specifically writing about boys' and girls' patterns of learning, there is no significance in our choice of 'he' or 'she'.

We wish you and your children every success in their secondary education.

Peter Downes and Carey Bennet

# CHAPTER ONE

# Choosing a secondary school

You've spent eleven years helping your child to grow and develop. Adolescence approaches and this new phase of your child's life is associated with the move to a new school.

A number of issues will affect the choice you make, such as:

- the schools within reasonable distance from home, and availability of transport
- the type of school: large or small, single-sex or coeducational, denominational or non-denominational, selective or non-selective
- your own opinion of the schools
- the availability of places.

In this chapter we will look at:

- the range of schools available
- finding out about a school
- what to look for on a visit
- admissions procedures.

# *The range of schools available*

## How much choice do you really have?

The great majority of parents choose to send their children to their local secondary school, and in a recent survey, over 90 per cent of parents said that they were either satisfied or very satisfied with their child's secondary school.

Of course, for those living in rural areas the choice may be limited; perhaps there is only one school within travelling distance. But the fact that parents are generally happy with their child's school suggests that the quality of the local school is the key, rather than the range of schools available.

In urban areas there may be several schools within reasonable distance, so parents need to decide which one they would like their child to attend.

Parents have *the right to express a preference* rather than absolute choice. You should be offered a place at your preferred school unless:

- it has already admitted pupils up to its limit
- it selects by ability and your child has not met the requirements
- it is denominational and has an agreement whereby it can limit the number of pupils who are not members of the same faith.

Between 80 and 95 per cent of parents are offered their first choice of school. Parents who are not offered the school they prefer have the right to appeal to an independent appeals committee. There has recently been a significant increase in the number of parents who go to appeal. More is said about this under **Admissions procedures** later in this chapter and there are further details in Appendix 1 at the end of the book.

# Different types of school

## *Age structures*

The most common pattern within the state education system is for children aged eleven to transfer to a secondary school which caters for pupils up to age sixteen or eighteen.

In some Local Education Authorities (LEAs) the pattern is different. For example, some have a First-Middle-Upper system with the Middle school serving pupils from seven or eight to thirteen or fourteen. Others have High Schools for 10/11 to 14-year-olds, followed by Upper Schools for 14 to 18-year-olds.

Where the secondary school serves pupils aged 11 to 16, there is usually a choice of school sixth form, sixth form college, or Further Education College at which students can take different types of Post-16 course (see Chapter 3 on Post-16 choices).

## *Denominational and non-denominational schools*

Denominational schools were set up to provide education within a particular Christian faith. This is reflected in the school's religious education and the daily act of worship, as well as in the everyday life of the school.

Most denominational secondary schools are either Church of England or Roman Catholic, but inter-denominational schools are also to be found, which provide an education in keeping with a range of Christian beliefs.

Families do not have to be members of the particular faith in order to attend a denominational school, but the school will usually give priority to baptised members and to regular church attenders. The school may ask for a letter from your local priest or minister to support an application on religious grounds. The requirements will be set out in the school's admissions information.

Most denominational secondary schools have Aided status. They come within the LEA, but unlike County schools, their governing bodies have total responsibility for their staff, school buildings, and admission arrangements (in consultation with the LEA).

There have been moves to establish state schools representing other religions, but none has so far been agreed by the Secretary of State.

Some schools within the LEA system are called Controlled schools. Many of these were originally founded by the Church. However, denominational Controlled schools do not necessarily apply religious criteria in their admissions.

## *Single-sex and coeducational schools*

Most secondary schools within the state sector are coeducational (mixed), providing for girls and boys. However, this does not mean that boys and girls are *always* taught together within mixed schools (see Chapter 4).

Where there are single-sex secondary schools in the area this provides greater choice for those parents who would prefer separate schooling for cultural, social or educational reasons.

The ethos and atmosphere of single-sex boys' and girls' schools tend to be different. Some parents value this, whilst others feel that a mix of girls and boys provides a more natural social setting.

In the past, boys' and girls' schools also offered quite different sorts of education. Today, the curriculum differences are fewer, partly because the National Curriculum determines much of what must be taught to all pupils, and partly because there is now a stronger emphasis on both boys and girls developing a broad range of skills and knowledge.

The general folklore is that pupils do better, academically, at single-sex schools, and this has been supported by analyses of GCSE examination results. However, a recent joint report by OFSTED (Office for Standards in Education) and the Equal Opportunities Commission concludes that

> *The comparison of single-sex and mixed schools is*
> *contentious and very complex; there is no*

*straightforward answer to whether one type of
school is more successful than the other because so
many variables are involved.*

It seems that much depends on factors such as parental support,
social class and the attainment of pupils on entry to the school.
Other studies suggest that teaching methods and the way pupils
are grouped are more important factors than whether the school is
single-sex or mixed. In other words, your child may do equally
well in a mixed school where teachers are alert to issues affecting
the progress of boys and girls, and when you are highly supportive
of the school and your child's education.

If you do have the choice, visiting the schools with your child
will give you a feel for the atmosphere and values of each, as well
as an opportunity to find out about boys' and girls' achievement
and social development.

## Selective and non-selective schools

The majority of secondary schools (about 90 per cent) have a comprehensive intake. This means that pupils are *not* selected on the
basis of ability.

Non-selective schools should not use any reference to ability
(such as tests or interviews to assess pupils' qualities) as part of
their admission arrangements.

In some areas a selective system is operated for some schools
(mainly the old grammar schools). Pupils usually sit a test which
measures their literacy, numeracy and verbal reasoning skills.
Children who score above a certain mark are eligible for a grammar school place. However, if there are not enough grammar
school places in the area, those with the highest scores may have
priority or other criteria may be applied (see **Admissions criteria**
later in this chapter).

Recently, schools which have had a comprehensive intake have
been allowed to select up to 10 per cent of pupils on the basis of

ability in a particular subject, such as Technology, Science, Languages or the Arts.

Proposals for the extension of selection are politically controversial. The Conservative Party would like to see more selection in pursuit of 'choice and diversity'. The Labour Party and the Liberal Democrats are more inclined to favour non-selective schools as a way of raising standards for all.

It is important to note here that nearly all secondary schools (whether selective or comprehensive), group and teach pupils according to ability at some stage and in some subjects (see Chapter 4).

## Technology Schools

There are currently about 180 Technology Schools in England. They are state schools (either Grant Maintained or LEA-run), and must teach the National Curriculum, but they give special emphasis to Technology, Science and Maths. They have been set up with the backing of commercial sponsorship and receive additional funding from central government.

## Language Colleges

Language Colleges are set up in a similar way to Technology Colleges but concentrate on Modern Foreign Languages. There are currently 42 of these schools nationally.

## City Technology Colleges (CTCs)

Fifteen CTCs were set up in the early 1990s, with funding from local businesses and central government. They are independent schools, but receive public funding and provide free education for pupils in the locality. CTCs provide an education with a strong emphasis on Technology. Pupils are selected on the basis of aptitude and enthusiasm for a Technology-based curriculum.

## Grant Maintained schools

Until the late 1980s all state schools came within the responsibility of the Local Education Authority. The 1988 Education Act made it possible for schools to become Grant Maintained by means of a parental ballot prompted by either the governing body or a petition from the parents of at least 20 per cent of the pupils.

About 15 per cent of secondary schools in England and Wales have become Grant Maintained (GM). Given that all schools now have considerable freedom to manage their affairs, including the management of their own finances, the main differences between GM and LEA schools are:

- GM schools are funded directly by central government through the Funding Agency for Schools (FAS).Their budgets are still linked to LEA funding but with additional money to meet their greater responsibilities.
- GM Governing Bodies are responsible for their admission arrangements (in agreement with the Secretary of State).
- GM schools are outside the Local Education Authority network (although they may be able to purchase some LEA services). They are accountable to their parents, as opposed to the LEA and parents.

## Special schools

Special schools provide for children who have special educational needs which cannot be met in a mainstream school. Many special schools cater for a wide range of special needs, but some are quite specialised, such as those for children with visual impairment or emotional and behavioural problems.

Parents cannot simply opt for a special school. Admission to a special school would normally follow a process of assessment of the child's needs referred to as 'Statutory Assessment'. This process may result in the production of a Statement which sets out what is needed to provide the child with an appropriate education. The

Statement should name a particular school. This is discussed further in Chapter 4.

## Independent schools

About 8 per cent of pupils in the United Kingdom are educated in independent schools. The first distinctive feature of such schools is that parents pay fees for their children and these vary according to the popularity and prestige of the school and whether or not their children are boarders (i.e. living in the school throughout the term), weekly boarders (returning home at weekends) or day pupils (usually returning home in the evening after doing supervised prep, or homework). Fees vary from about £4,000 per year up to over £12,000. Most schools offer scholarships or bursaries to attract particularly able pupils whose parents cannot afford the fees. The Government Assisted Places Scheme (address at the end of this chapter) assists with the fees of some 38,000 pupils at independent schools. The level of financial support offered by the Scheme varies according to the personal circumstances of the family.

The Assisted Places Scheme is politically controversial: the Conservative Party wishes to extend it, the Labour Party would abolish it and the Liberal Democrats would replace it by allowing LEAs to buy places at independent schools where this would best meet a pupil's needs. All parties state that no child who has already been given an assisted place will be deprived of it during their educational career.

The second distinctive feature of independent schools is that they can select their pupils by examination and/or by interview. Although in many cases this may lead to social and academic elitism, some independent schools specialise in taking pupils with lower ability or with behavioural problems. Some offer specialist opportunities for musicians and dancers with outstanding ability and dedication.

Being independent, these schools may follow their own curriculum but in practice the National Curriculum is closely adhered to, sometimes with additions such as Latin, a second or third foreign language and more opportunities for sport.

Independent schools tend to have significantly smaller classes than state schools and this can provide more individual attention for pupils which, other things being equal, should help them to achieve better results. The questions you may want to ask are:

- Is the difference between what your child would achieve in an independent school and a state school worth the money?
- What else could you spend that money on for her benefit (such as musical instruments and lessons, books, computers or travel abroad)?

If you are considering independent education you can obtain advice from the Independent Schools Information Service (ISIS) whose address is to be found at the end of this chapter. If your interest in the independent sector is based upon the need for boarding, you might not be aware that there are state boarding schools where the boarding fees are much lower than at independent schools. Details can be obtained from the State Boarding Schools Information Service (STABIS).

A full discussion of the merits of independent education is beyond the scope of this book. Your decision will depend upon your financial circumstances, both now and for the next seven years, and upon your assessment of the state schools within travelling distance. Most of the advice in this book is equally valid whether you opt for state or independent education.

## Home schooling

A small number of parents decide to educate their children themselves or with others, outside the school system.

Parents are obliged by law to ensure that their child receives 'efficient full-time education suitable to his or her age, ability and aptitude', either by attendance at a school 'or otherwise'.

If you remove your child from a school you must inform the LEA. If you have taught your child at home from the start you are not obliged to do so, but you may find that you get some helpful advice from the LEA. The LEA will monitor what is being provided. You do not have to follow the National Curriculum, but some parents find it a useful framework.

Parents may opt for home schooling for a number of reasons:

- a desire to focus on their child's particular talents and interests
- because of problems with socialising, school phobia or bullying
- or simply because they are not in sympathy with the aims or organisation of the education system.

Whatever the reason, this is a big commitment. Parents need to think very carefully about:

- their ability to provide appropriate and stimulating experiences on a long-term basis
- the child's need for the company of others, for their social and intellectual development
- the question of examinations, qualifications, and future career requirements.

Advice and support for parents thinking about home schooling is available from Education Otherwise (address at the end of the chapter) and from your Local Education Authority.

# Finding out about a school

Recent surveys have shown that distance from home and the child's own preference are factors which strongly influence parents' choice of secondary school. These are important considerations as they relate to practical and emotional aspects which may ease your child's move to secondary school. You may not want to follow blindly your child's wishes but it is important to talk about the possibilities and involve him or her in the decision-making.

More and more, parents are looking at other factors before they make their choice, such as exam performance, extra-curricular activities and the ethos or atmosphere of the school.

The range of information now available about each school can be quite daunting. Some sources of information include:

- the views of other parents and pupils
- the school's own prospectus
- exam league tables
- the OFSTED inspection report
- your own observations.

In the following section we look at these sources of information, and different points for you to consider, leaving till last the most important – your visit to the school.

## Using sources of information about a school

### Other parents' views

The surveys referred to above show that other parents' views strongly influence parents' choice of school.

These views can certainly be illuminating, but remember that other parents' feelings about the school will be based on their own and their children's particular experiences of school, which may or may not be similar to yours. If you are seeking other parents' views, ask a range of parents. If you would like to talk to a parent Governor of the school, the names can be found in the Annual Report to Parents, or can be obtained from the school office.

If you are seeking the views of pupils, ask them *why* they hold the particular views they do.

Remember also that whilst schools change, reputations linger on! Make sure your informants are up-to-date.

## *The school prospectus*

Schools are now required by law to publish a prospectus each year. The prospectus must include (amongst many other things):

- the school's principles and values
- details about the school's policies on dealing with complaints, special educational needs, sex education, charging for activities, careers education and other areas
- National Curriculum assessment results (of pupils in Year 9)
- Public examination results for GCSE, GCE A Level and AS Level, and vocational courses
- the destinations of its school leavers
- pupil absence rates.

The prospectus should begin to give you a picture of the school but you may find it hard to make sense of some of the information, such as the exam results and absence rates.

As a yardstick for judging pupil absences, OFSTED regards absence rates of more than 10 per cent of possible attendance as worrying. The difficulty here is that schools have different approaches to recording pupils' authorised and unauthorised absences. Very low absence rates could reflect a relaxed interpretation of what is an unauthorised absence.

Perhaps the key question is, are attendance rates and exam results improving year by year?

## *Exam league tables*

In addition to each school providing its own exam results in the prospectus, the Department for Education and Employment publishes a league table of all schools' results, county by county. These are distributed in the Autumn term to parents with children who are due to transfer to secondary school the following year.

Although they make interesting headlines, there are a number of problems with exam league tables as a way of comparing schools:

- Children and schools do not have the same starting points. They differ in terms of ability, selective or comprehensive intake, local area, facilities and parental support for their children's learning.
- Results need to be seen over a period of time to see whether they are typical for the school, and whether they are improving or on the decline.
- Results can be affected by factors beyond the school's control, such as very high staff turnover in a particular year, a disaster which has disrupted the school, or the creation of a nearby selective school which may cream off the brightest children.

## OFSTED inspection report

All secondary schools will have undergone an OFSTED inspection. This is a full inspection of the school by an external team of inspectors appointed by the Office for Standards in Education. At the end of the inspection a detailed report is produced, as well as a brief summary for parents. A copy of the report should be lodged at the local library. Copies can also be requested (for the copying charge) from the school.

The report (and the summary) describe the strengths and weaknesses of the school as observed by the OFSTED team. They also say what aspects of the school should now be improved or developed.

## Visiting the school

Prospectuses, others parents' views, OFSTED reports and league tables will provide a mountain of information about a school and may suggest things you want to find out more about. We would suggest that the most valuable source of all is visiting the school and talking to staff and pupils. The impression given by glossy brochures can then be tested against your first-hand observations.

Most schools offer opportunities such as open days or evenings and special meetings for prospective parents. If it is not too burdensome on the school, more than one visit is helpful, and a visit during the school day is particularly useful.

# What to look for on a visit

Below are some suggestions for further questions and observations . . . but also a warning!

It is not realistic to expect to find out everything there is to know about the school. There are hundreds of questions that you *could* ask – but decide what matters most to you, and ask your child what is important to him.

## Focus above all on the people

### The Headteacher and senior staff

- Do these key staff express a clear vision and aims for the school and its pupils?
- From what you see, do they appear to have good relationships with pupils and do they relate warmly and positively to you as parents?
- Do they describe how the school would like to work with you as parents in the education of your child?

### The staff

- How do the teachers and other staff talk to pupils? Are staff enthusiastic about the pupils as well as about their subjects?

### The pupils

- Are pupils confident, friendly to visitors, interested in their work, able to speak positively about the school (as well as issuing the predictable moans)?

## Ethos and positive behaviour

Does the school's approach emphasise the celebration of success and achievement? Is there an agreed policy on promoting positive behaviour, as well as responding to poor behaviour? How are parents involved?

Has the school taken positive steps regarding difficult issues such as bullying, equal opportunities, racism, drugs? How are parents involved and informed about these issues?

What is the school's policy on school dress? If there is a uniform, ask about the reasons for it and the importance attached to it. Do not assume that the absence of uniform means lack of order or discipline – or vice versa!

## The school buildings and facilities

Try not to judge a secondary school purely on the quality of its buildings. Instead, see whether buildings are used and maintained to their maximum for the education of the pupils. It says more for the school to see dated buildings used to excellent effect, than new facilities under-used to preserve their appearance.

You could ask about the school's approach to replacement and development of facilities and equipment, and whether there are any major projects on the horizon.

Does the school environment look cared for and tidy? Ask who is responsible for keeping it a pleasant place. Do members of staff have specific responsibilities or do classes or year groups take care of different areas? Are pupils involved through the curriculum or otherwise in designing, changing or maintaining their environment? Is litter-picking a punishment?

Are there attractive and engaging displays in teaching areas, corridors and other spaces?

Is the building parent-friendly – welcoming, with clear instructions and directions, a comfortable place to wait, and accessible reception and information facilities?

Is it pupil-friendly – for example do pupils have places to sit and to keep belongings?

## Aspects of the curriculum

Sometimes parents find that what is taught in schools today, and the language used to describe it, has changed so much from when they were at school that teachers' descriptions are hard to follow.

If you find yourself confused by educational jargon – say so! You will probably not be the only one! We have provided an explanation of the most frequently used abbreviations and terms in Appendix 10.

It may be most helpful to ask about the *aims* of the curriculum – in other words, what the school wants its pupils to learn and why it organises subjects in that particular way. Answers to such questions should give you a feel for what the school values and is trying to achieve.

Although you will no doubt want the school to be good at everything, you may want to ask what, in the school's view, are its particular strengths. Remember that 'strong' and 'weak' departments may change with the arrival or departure of key staff, new facilities or staff training.

You may want to explore the school's commitment to *all* their pupils' success, (not just the very bright or the less able). What do they do to ensure that each pupil is doing as well as she can? How does the school measure this?

Most parents want a good all-round education for their child and look for achievement across a wide range of academic and non-academic areas within the formal curriculum, extra-curricular activities and work in the community.

## Extra-curricular activities

There is enormous variety in what schools can and do provide beyond the formal curriculum. Find out what is on offer. Also ask what the school does to encourage all its pupils to participate in these activities. More is said about this in Chapter 5.

# Class size

Few schools are in a position to create small classes across all age groups and it is thought that marginal variations (for example, between 28 and 30) make little difference to the quality of education. The important questions to ask are about how the school uses different teaching methods to meet the learning needs of their pupils – whether very able, of average ability or with learning difficulties.

# Homework

Is there an agreed school policy on the sorts of tasks set, and the amount of time pupils of different ages are expected to spend on homework? Does the school have a system (homework timetable, homework record books) which avoids overloading (or under-loading)? Is there a homework club or place to do homework after school? How are parents encouraged to be involved (see Chapter 4)?

# Parental involvement

This important issue is discussed in more detail in Chapter 6.
At this stage you may want to explore:

- how the school keeps parents informed about their child's progress
- how they see you as contributing to your child's learning
- how parents are involved more broadly in school life
- whether the school makes opportunities to inform parents about educational issues and changes.

# Pastoral organisation

The pastoral side of the school refers to aspects of its organisation (such as 'Year Head', 'tutor group', 'house system', 'lower/upper school') which help to ensure the welfare, well-being and personal development of pupils.

Different schools use different approaches to pastoral organisation. No particular approach is best. The important issue is whether it provides a happy, secure learning environment. Do some members of staff know each child well and have oversight of his academic and social development? How clear are the routes for pupils and parents to raise issues that concern them?

These are just suggestions. Some important things on a visit to a school are:

- to be an active listener and observer
- not to be afraid to ask about what matters to you
- to look for the positive rather than only looking for things which confirm your fears or prejudices about the school.

# Admission procedures

## Information for parents

The Local Education Authority is responsible for the admission of pupils to LEA schools. After the allocation of places, most tasks relating to the move from primary to secondary school (or transfer at other times) will be handled by the school. In Aided and Grant Maintained schools the responsibility for pupil admissions lies with the governing body of the school.

Each LEA must publish information for parents about the LEA schools in its area, and its admission arrangements. Parents of pupils in Year 6 generally receive this information in the second half of the Autumn term, when they are usually asked to express their preference for a secondary school.

Grant Maintained schools will provide local parents with information on their admission procedures. Some do this directly through the primary schools; others may have an arrangement where they publish their information within the LEA's booklet.

If you are interested in a school in another local authority, contact that authority's main education offices and ask for their admissions information. A decision by the Law Lords in 1989 called the Greenwich Judgement means that LEAs cannot refuse a place at a school purely on the grounds that the pupil lives outside the LEA area.

## Admissions criteria

The information provided for parents will include the rules which apply in allocating places at each school. These are referred to as the *admissions criteria*. Admissions criteria are used when the number of pupils seeking a place at a school is greater than the number of places that can be offered. The following are examples of common admissions criteria :

- living within a defined catchment area
- distance from home to school
- the attendance of a brother or sister at the school
- attendance at named primary schools
- special educational or medical grounds.

Denominational schools usually have admissions criteria such as giving priority to:

- children of practising Roman Catholic or Church of England families
- children attending Roman Catholic or Church of England primary schools in the area.

Selective schools will include criteria which refer to performance in specified tests, or other methods of judging ability or aptitude in a particular subject area.

Schools and LEAs cannot refuse a place to a child solely on the grounds that the child has behaviour problems. This is of particular relevance to pupils seeking admission to a school after permanent exclusion from another (see Chapter 8).

## Admission limits

Schools must admit pupils up to the admission limit published in the information for parents. Sometimes this number will be referred to as the 'standard number'. After they have reached their published admission limit they can refuse admission if, by taking more pupils, this would affect the quality of education at the school, or would be an inefficient use of resources.

Denominational schools can admit below their published admission limit (if they have an agreement with the LEA) in order to preserve their character as a school representing a particular faith.

Selective schools can admit below their published admission limit if not enough pupils achieve the required standard in their selection tests.

## Expressing a preference

Each education authority has its own system for organising admissions. The information for parents describes what you must do to state your preferred school(s), and by when. This will usually be by the end of the Autumn term, so you do need to start thinking about the options at least by the beginning of that term, if not sooner.

You will usually be asked to return a form either via the primary school or directly to the LEA. In some LEAs you do not have to do this if the school you want is your catchment area school.

You may be asked to list a number of schools in order of preference. Try to find out whether, by naming a very popular school as a first preference, you may lessen the chance of being offered a place at your second preference or your local school. You can find out more about this from your local Education Office, or by attending any information evenings organised by the school or LEA.

It is sensible to get some idea of your chances of gaining a place at your preferred school, and to warn your child if the chances are slim.

If you are applying to one or more Grant Maintained schools you may find that you have to complete a separate form for each. However, in some areas the LEA and GM schools co-operate to use a single system.

It is very important to follow the instructions and advice provided by the LEA or school. If you do not return the correct form, or if it is late, you might not be offered the school you want.

If you need help, telephone your local Education Office and ask for advice.

## Hearing the news

Most parents are offered their first choice of school. You are more likely to get your first choice when it is your nearest or catchment area school.

You should hear which school your child has been allocated during the Spring or early in the Summer term. You may be asked to confirm that you want the place. Do this promptly either to ensure your place or so that it can be offered to another child if you don't want it. If at a later stage you no longer want the place, always tell the LEA or the school; another child may be waiting for that place.

If a school is oversubscribed, a waiting list or reserve list will be drawn up. If places become available later (for instance, through people moving out of the area) they will be offered to pupils on the list, in order of the admissions criteria.

Once offered, a place cannot be withdrawn, unless applied for fraudulently or not accepted within a reasonable time-scale.

## Appeals

Parents whose request for a place has been turned down by the Local Education Authority (or by the governing body of an Aided or Grant Maintained school) have the right to appeal against this decision to an independent appeals committee. This process is described in detail in Appendix 1.

There is no right of appeal for City Technology Colleges, but parents can write to the governing body if they feel that a decision was unfair.

## Be positive!

If, in the end, you do not get a place at the school you most wanted, do not be too downhearted. Remember that most parents are happy with their child's secondary school, and most schools are industrious places where the staff want the very best for their pupils – just as you do for your child.

Even if you are disappointed, it is important that you are not negative with your child about her next school. A positive outlook and good communications between you and the school will contribute to her happiness and success.

Whatever school she attends, it is the way you both approach school life which will make the difference. The rest of this book will show you how to help your child make the most of her school career.

# *Further reading*

**Home education pack,** Advisory Centre for Education and Education Now, for parents considering educating their children at home.

**Parents and Grant Maintained Schools,** Advisory Centre for Education, in the 'My child in school' series.

**School choice and appeals** (2nd edition, 1994), Advisory Centre for Education, ISBN 0 900029 85 4.

# Useful organisations

**The Admissions Team,** DfEE, will take queries on LEA or GM school admission issues. Contact it at: Schools 1B, Department for Education and Employment, Sanctuary Buildings, Great Smith Street, London SW1P 3BT. Tel: 0171 925 6474.

**Advisory Centre for Education (ACE) Ltd** provides information on all aspects of secondary education. It is at 1b Aberdeen Studios, 22–24 Highbury Grove, London N5 2DQ. Tel: 0171 354 8321 (publications); 0171 354 8321 (advice, between 2 and 5pm).

**Assisted Places Team,** Mowden Hall, Staindrop Road, Darlington, DL3 9BG. Tel: 01325 392163 or 392177.

**Boarding Schools Association,** Ysgol Nant, Valley Road, Llanfairfechan, Gwynedd, LL33 0ES. Tel. and fax: 01248 680542.

**Education Otherwise,** PO Box 7420, London, N9 9SG. Enquiry line: 0891 518303.

**The Grant Maintained Schools Centre,** Wesley Court, Priory Road, High Wycombe, Bucks, HP13 6SE. Tel: 01494 474470.

**The Grant Maintained Schools Foundation,** 36 Great Smith Street, London, SW1P 3BU. Tel: 0171 799 2660.

**Independent Schools Information Service (ISIS),** 56 Buckingham Gate, London SW1E 6AG. Tel: 0171 630 8793/4.

**State Boarding Schools Information Service (STABIS),** same address as the Boarding Schools Association.

# CHAPTER TWO

# Settling in to a new school

However old or young you are, whenever you move to a new setting – a new place of work, a new home, a new school – there is always a mixture of excitement and anxiety. This is especially true of eleven year old children moving into their new secondary school.

In this chapter we will be looking at:

- initial contacts with secondary school
- the journey to school
- daily routines
- coping with new pressures
- establishing good work patterns
- clothing, equipment and charges
- making new friends
- finding out whom to contact.

# Initial contacts with secondary school

The good news is that the vast majority of children settle down quickly and happily. Parents need to be reassured themselves so that they can help their children feel happy about the move. You may have unhappy memories of the first days and weeks you spent in your secondary school a generation ago but the situation today is very much better.

This is because good schools go to great lengths to make sure that their new pupils settle in happily. They often do this by visiting them in their primary schools and by having them into the secondary school for a Taster Day before the end of the summer term.

Many schools offer parents the opportunity to look around with their child and some will give you the chance to have a short personal meeting with one of the teachers. It is particularly important for you to talk to a teacher at the new school, possibly the form tutor or Head of Year, if your child is timid, likely to be easily upset or is afraid of being bullied. Advance warning of possible difficulties enables the teachers to be ready with any support that may be needed.

Sometimes parents who already have a child at the secondary school think that they do not need to go to these transfer meetings because they already know all about the school. There are two good reasons why you should still make every effort to go: firstly, schools are always changing and there may be new ideas, curriculum or practical procedures which are different from the ones you knew about with your older children, and there will certainly be different members of staff; secondly, although *you* may have been through all this before, it is a unique experience for each child in the family and younger children do not want to feel devalued. Your attendance at the transfer meetings gives your child the message that his education matters to you.

Although you can be reassured that, on the whole, everything will go well, there are some aspects of the early weeks of which you need to be aware so that you can take the right steps to give your child a good start.

# The journey to school

For most pupils, the journey to primary school has been relatively short and easy. The journey to secondary school may well involve public transport, or using specially provided buses, or a longer walk or a cycle ride. The practical problem of getting to school on time is one of the anxieties faced by Year 7 pupils, and parents can do something to help.

Where possible, it is a good idea to practise the journey a day or two before your child actually has to make it. Look out for any difficult road crossings or bus changes. Try to find at least one other neighbouring pupil who is going to the same school so that your child has a travelling companion.

If the Local Education Authority (LEA) provides transport, make sure that you have applied for a bus pass in good time and impress on your child the importance of keeping it in a safe place. Bus drivers do actually inspect passes, either daily or from time to time, and have the power to refuse to accept pupils without a pass, although this is usually waived if there is a teacher at the bus-queue who can plead on the child's behalf. Make sure your child always carries enough money either to get alternative transport home or to be able to ring for help if needed. This should be quite separate from any money for buying lunch or for spending on refreshments.

Some parents have told us that the journeys on the school bus are the part of the day which new pupils enjoy least. Every school has rules about behaviour on buses, of course, but these are difficult to enforce. On most buses there is no adult supervision and the driver may be too busy concentrating on the traffic to have detailed oversight of what is going on behind or upstairs.

## SETTLING IN TO A NEW SCHOOL

The enforcement of discipline on buses is a grey area. Schools clearly want and expect their pupils to behave well, and lay down what standards are expected, but it is the LEA which is actually responsible for the safe transportation of the pupils on buses provided by them. Some schools put an expectation on older pupils that they will report any misbehaviour and this can work well. It is a good idea for your child to sit with a group of friends of the same age if possible and not to act provocatively towards older pupils. If there are instances of misbehaviour or bullying on the bus, it is best to report the matter quickly to the school rather than allowing a problem to develop. Always be specific about the incident and, where possible, give the date and time of the incident and the names of pupils behaving badly. Schools have the authority to punish pupils for bad behaviour on buses and the ultimate sanction is for a pupil not to be allowed to travel on LEA-provided buses. This causes a great deal of trouble to parents so it is wise to instil in your child from day one that good behaviour on the bus is as important as it is within school.

More and more parents take their children to school by car. This is understandable, given anxieties about danger from traffic and from potential physical threat. Our advice, however, would be to try to keep car use to a minimum. School entrances and nearby streets can be extremely congested at the beginning and the end of the day and the more parents try to drop their children at the school gate, the worse this becomes. If you do have to use the car, consider dropping your child at some distance from the school so that she walks the last stretch. Another reason for not over-using the car is that it increases your child's dependency on you. Learning to cope with a journey and with the practicalities of public transport is an important lesson for young people. Although you would never want to let your child walk alone through a potentially dangerous area, it is a good idea for her to walk at least part of the way to school. There is increasing concern among medical specialists about the lack of exercise undertaken by young people and a brisk walk each day is in the best interests of your child's health.

# Daily routines

## A good start to the day

You and your child can avoid many pressures and much unhappiness by being well-organised in the mornings. It is important that your child gets up early enough to have a good breakfast. Recent research has shown that pupils who do not have any breakfast perform less well academically than those who do. They tend to snack in between lessons and to have run out of mental energy long before lunch-time. Personal tastes for breakfast will differ as will cultural habits but some combination of fruit, cereal, toast and a drink are strongly recommended by dietitians.

Other research has shown that it is not a good idea for children to watch breakfast television. It encourages a short attention span which makes it more difficult for children to concentrate. Some breakfast television programmes jump quickly from subject to subject so that children are too hyped up to focus on lessons when they get to school.

If your child packs her school bag the night before, you will probably all have a calmer start to the day. Check the timetable to see that she has all materials for lessons the following day, including PE kit and items needed for Technology. If she is taking a packed lunch rather than buying lunch at school (see Chapter 5), allow time for the lunch to be prepared and encourage her to do at least part of the preparation herself. Check that she has any money needed for the journey, for lunch and the 'emergency money' already mentioned.

# Coping with new pressures

Children's responses to starting at a new school vary widely. Most are excited and enjoy it thoroughly from the moment the term begins; others are anxious. What is generally agreed by all the parents and pupils we have talked to is that new Year 7 pupils get very much more tired than they did at primary school.

This is understandable because they will probably be doing more walking around the school site in order to go to specialist classrooms, they will be changing subject and teacher several times during the day (rather than having mainly one teacher as they did in the primary school), and they may well be starting new subjects, such as foreign languages, and tackling more demanding work than they did in the last stages of their previous school.

Now that there is much better communication between primary and secondary schools because of the National Curriculum, the former practice of allowing an easy settling-in period in secondary school work is less common. Children get on to new work quite quickly and will probably be set homework from the beginning. Tackling homework is dealt with more fully in Chapter 4.

What is universally agreed is that Year 7 pupils starting in their new school need plenty of sleep. You need to be alert to the possibility that the excitement and different pressures of a new and much larger school may make your child more short-tempered than usual. At the end of the school day, many will want to unwind or just talk to you about all the things that have happened during the day, before getting down to homework. If your child does not want to talk much, don't become too aggressive in interrogating her. Over-anxious questioning about 'how did you get on at school today?' is not the best way to let children unburden themselves. Wait for them to open up and then listen sympathetically.

# Establishing good work patterns

The need for good personal organisation has already been mentioned but it needs to extend beyond the practicalities of the start of the school day. Most secondary schools now give their pupils specific training in personal organisation, either during tutor group time or through a course – probably entitled Personal and Social Education (PSE) (see Chapter 3 for further details).

This training may well include the use of a day book, in which pupils note the lessons for each day of the week, the homework set, and any other special requirements (for example, ingredients for food preparation in Technology, PE kit, musical instrument for school band rehearsal). The day book may also be used to send messages home about forthcoming events. Some schools use a day book which has a section for a response from parents (such as an acknowledgement that a letter home has been received).

Other schools take the day book a stage further by using it as a means of sending comments home to parents about how their children are getting on. They may well ask you to sign it regularly. It is important that you support your child in settling into good routines from the very beginning of her time in secondary school. When you sign the day-book regularly and send back reply-slips to letters on time, you are sending a clear message to your child about the process of education and about your commitment to her and to the school.

Pupils often make the mistake of not noting down in sufficient detail what they are supposed to do for homework. This is sometimes the fault of teachers who leave the setting of the homework until the last minute of the lesson and do it too hastily. Quite often, children make notes on homework which seemed clear at the time but which are too brief by the time they have got home. This is an aspect of personal organisation which needs practice but is well worth it in the long run.

## Personal planning

Secondary school subjects use a combination of text books, exercise books, work sheets and folders and it is important for your child to have the right material for each day. Some schools provide lockers where children can keep books they do not need. Some children prefer to carry all their books around with them, out of anxiety at suddenly finding they have not got what they need. Children have been known to carry round enough files and blank paper to write an entire book! This should be discouraged – it often means that quite small children are carrying bags which are too heavy for them and causing potential damage to their backs (see Chapter 5 for more advice on health). It also means that text books are getting damaged by being squashed into bags. A far better method is for pupils to keep their books at home and take only what they need for the day – but this does require time and planning.

The pattern of secondary school life, packing up and moving belongings around the school several times a day, offers lots of opportunities for losing things. If your child has a habit of leaving things everywhere she goes, now is the time to make a fresh start. Establish new routines for checking that she has all her belongings with her. It is important too to label items of clothing and equipment. This increases the chances of lost property being found, provided your child knows the school routine for tracking down lost items. Better by far not to lose things in the first place.

# Clothing, equipment and charges

## Uniform

The school prospectus will tell you about the expectations in relation to uniform. Most secondary schools have a dress code specifying what must be worn. Many have adopted unisex sweatshirts while others still retain the traditional blazers and ties for boys and formal dresses for girls. Year 7 pupils are usually very pleased to see themselves in their new uniform and are proud of this identification with their new school. The school's regulations may also specify what may be worn by way of jewellery and make-up. It is normal for schools to make these expectations of pupils and you are strongly advised to adhere to the regulations. Pupils who start to test the boundaries of what may or may not be permitted get into a lot of unnecessary trouble so it is a good idea to discourage your child from this kind of behaviour, not only at the beginning of their time in the new school but throughout their career. Do not be misled by your child's claims that 'everybody else is wearing four nose-studs and getting away with it'. This is usually a tactic adopted by children who want to express their individuality. There are many other more acceptable ways of being an individual in school – doing excellent work, being creative, imaginative and responsive in class, joining in lots of clubs, initiating new activities – which create much less trouble for the teachers and the pupils and, in the long run, for you as parents. Uniform is an ancient battle-ground over which it is simply not worth fighting.

## Equipment

The school prospectus will also specify what basic equipment the school would like you to provide for your child. Although education in the United Kingdom is technically free, there is an understanding that parents will provide pens, pencils, rubbers and a simple set of mathematical instruments. Some schools go further and ask parents to buy a simple calculator, an English dictionary and a foreign language dictionary. Exercise books are usually provided by the school. Text books are also provided free but there may not be enough money available in the school for every pupil to have a book for every subject. If your child is fortunate enough to have his own text book to bring home to do homework, make sure he looks after it and does not damage it stuffing it into a schoolbag full of games kit. More and more schools are asking for voluntary parental contributions towards the cost of text books and you will obviously make your own decision as to whether or not you wish to support the school in this way. The important thing to remember is that contributions of this kind are entirely voluntary.

# Charges

From time to time, your child may be asked to make a small financial contribution towards the cost of materials used in Art, Pottery, Craft, Design and Technology, Textiles and Food Technology. If you do so, your child becomes the owner of the items produced and can bring them home at the end of the project. It is not advisable to rely on the products of your son's Food Technology class for your evening meal, however excellent a cook he may be. If the relevant teacher has been absent, or if there is a power cut, you may go hungry!

As for other charges, every school prospectus has to include details of the charging and remissions policy approved by the Governors. This will tell you that trips and study visits undertaken mainly in school time as part of the curriculum are free but that voluntary contributions are invited. In these days of financial difficulties for schools, the school has to reserve the right to cancel the trip if not enough 'voluntary' contributions are forthcoming. Parents can be charged the board and lodging element of a residential trip undertaken within or outside school time as part of the curriculum. If you qualify for Family Credit or Income Support, you cannot be charged or expected to make a voluntary contribution. Schools can charge for the full cost of optional activities which take place mainly outside school hours.

Schools have varying policies on charging for music lessons. Pupils taking a GCSE or Advanced Level course cannot be charged for instrumental lessons which form part of that course. A charge can be made for music tuition provided in school time either individually or in groups of not more than four. More often than not, younger pupils take lessons in small groups at a subsidised rate so that costs for beginners can be kept low until it becomes clear that they want to continue with the instrument. The Head of Music at your child's school will be able to give you the details.

There are a number of ways in which parents facing financial hardship can obtain help with their children's education and more details will be found in Chapter 9.

# *Making new friends*

One of the main anxieties experienced by Year 7 pupils is the fear of having no friends. This is obviously most acute for a child who is the only one transferring from a particular primary school. Be reassured – eleven-year-olds are remarkably flexible in making new friends. Even those who have come with a group of friends from a previous school will soon be making new friends.

Good schools have a number of ways of helping new pupils to get to know each other. The tutor will make sure that nobody feels left out – but for this to work does require an effort of openness on the part of the pupils. It is not a good idea for your child to cling too closely to a friend from their last school. It is quite common for children of this age to become friends and then fall out within days or even hours. There is no need to be alarmed by this. Encourage your child to get to know as many class-mates as possible, to talk to you about them if she wants to and, in due course, to come round to each other's houses after school or at weekends, if circumstances permit. Discourage your child from being over-reliant on a small clique of friends. Year 7 girls are particularly inclined to form little friendship groups and then exclude others in a way which can be hurtful.

# *Finding out whom to contact*

One of the earliest challenges for you as a new parent is to find out which teacher is the most appropriate one to contact if you have any problems. We shall be looking at this in more detail in Chapter 8 but even at this early stage, try to find out the names and responsibilities of the key teachers in your child's life.

The school may well send out an explanatory leaflet to guide you. The person your child will see most often, usually twice a day

## SETTLING IN TO A NEW SCHOOL

for registration, will be the form tutor and it is she to whom every-day matters (absence notes, requests for time off for doctor's appointments, etc.) should usually be sent. Any minor problems can usually be dealt with by the form tutor, provided she knows quickly when something is worrying your son or daughter.

Depending on what pastoral system the school operates, the next person in terms of seniority may be a Head of Year or a Head of House. This teacher may become involved if there are more serious problems of discipline or bullying, or if a pupil is not set-tling down to work as she should.

If your child is having difficulty with a particular subject, it may be best to write to the subject teacher. In secondary schools, sub-ject teachers are organised into departments (English, Mathematics, etc.) or sometimes into faculties (Humanities, Sciences, Design subjects) and there will be a Head of Department or Faculty who will take responsibility for what your child learns in class. In some situations you may need to make contact with the Head of Department.

Depending on how your child's school is organised, a Deputy Head may have overall responsibility for the pastoral or academic teams of teachers. Some schools do not have a division of this kind but have a Deputy Head with overall responsibility, academic and pastoral, for a section of the school such as Years 7 to 9, Years 10 and 11. Find out who the Deputy is for the section of the school to which your child belongs.

One of the biggest differences between the primary and sec-ondary school is the Headteacher's detailed knowledge of your child. It is unlikely that a secondary Headteacher would know your child in sufficient depth to be able to give an immediate answer to a query about her. Do not be surprised if a letter sent to the Head comes back with an answer supplied by somebody else.

It is worth finding out about the structures within your child's school so that you can talk to the appropriate person on any mat-ter. This will almost certainly be explained to you at meetings before your child transfers, or in the school prospectus.

# Final thoughts

The process of transfer from primary to secondary school may seem daunting, especially if it involves your oldest child and you are experiencing it for the first time. In this chapter we have suggested how you can avoid or reduce some of the pressures and difficulties.

We need to say again that the vast majority of Year 7 pupils settle in very well, enjoy the new challenges and go on to do well in their new school. You can play a part by keeping calm, helping your child to be methodical and by giving positive support and reassurance if it is needed.

Enjoy the experience yourself. If you share in the excitement and challenge of your child's secondary education, you may perhaps be able to revise some of the knowledge you once had, many years ago, and you will find that there are a lot of new things to learn too.

# Further reading

**Primary-secondary transfer,** Advisory Centre for Education, in the 'My child in school' series. (See Appendix 12 for address.)

# CHAPTER THREE

# The journey through the secondary school

In this chapter you will be able find out about the subjects your child will study throughout her time in secondary school and how you can help her at the turning-points in her career where decisions have to be made.

We shall be looking at:

- the National Curriculum
- Key Stage 3
- Key Stage 4
- education beyond 16.

It can be difficult for parents with a child in secondary school now to realise how much things have changed since they were at school and how they are continuing to change. A good school will keep you fully informed about the curriculum and the choices to be made. If at any time you feel that the information provided is unclear, insist politely on receiving a better explanation.

The secondary school life-cycle falls into three phases:

- Key Stage 3 (Years 7 to 9) for pupils aged 11 to 14
- Key Stage 4 (Years 10 and 11) for pupils aged 14 to 16
- Post-16 (not yet called Key Stage 5) for students aged 16 to 19 who continue in education beyond the age when they are allowed to leave school.

Most secondary schools take pupils in the 11 to 16 age range or 11 to 18 if they have their own Sixth Form. In some areas of the country there are Middle Schools from which children transfer after Year 7, or after Year 8. In other areas there are High Schools which teach pupils until the end of Key Stage 3 when they transfer to Upper School.

# *The National Curriculum*

Until 1988 every school had its own curriculum. In theory, the teachers could decide what to teach and for how long. Looking back, it sounds chaotic, but in practice most schools taught roughly the same subjects for the same length of time because they were all preparing pupils for the same examinations at 16+ . In a sense, the Exam Boards dictated what was taught in schools.

The 1988 Education Act aimed to enforce greater consistency by laying down a National Curriculum which specifies what subjects have to be taught and what should be taught in each subject. Pupils in all state-funded schools (LEA or Grant Maintained) are covered by the National Curriculum requirements. Pupils in independent schools are not affected by this law but in practice most independent schools follow the National Curriculum fairly closely. There are some slight differences for schools in Wales, and schools in Scotland and Northern Ireland have different arrangements.

The first version of the National Curriculum proved to be unworkable. All the subject specialists involved in drawing up the National Curriculum Orders had simply been too enthusiastic in cramming as much as possible into their part of the curriculum.

The Dearing Committee revised the curriculum and the 1995 version reduced the specified content in many of the subjects and allowed some flexibility for pupils to choose what they want to do (see later). The 1995 National Curriculum lasts at least until the year 2000. It may be revised again to meet the changing needs of young people and society.

The jargon of the National Curriculum can be slightly confusing at first sight. Fortunately, the traditional idea of a *subject* has not disappeared but some are designated as *core subjects* and others as *foundation subjects*. The three core subjects which all pupils have to study up to the end of Key Stage 4 are:

- English
- Mathematics
- Science.

These are the three subjects which are formally tested at 14+, the end of Key Stage 3.

The foundation subjects are:

- Technology
- Physical Education    } compulsory up to 16
- Modern Languages
- History
- Geography
- Art    } optional in Key Stage 4
- Music.

Religious Education is compulsory for all pupils and sex education must also be included in the curriculum.

At each Key Stage the *Programmes of Study* (PoS) define what children will be taught. There is naturally some debate over what has been put in and what has been left out. There is nothing to stop teachers adding to the Programmes of Study if they wish but in practice there is usually such a lot of material to be covered that they have to work themselves and their pupils hard to cover the ground. Many schools make available to pupils the Programmes of Study in each subject so that parents who wish to can do some background reading for themselves and can at least know what their children are studying.

Another new piece of terminology is *Attainment Targets (AT)*. These are the broad headings under which pupils' learning is grouped. In English, for example, AT1 is Speaking and Listening, AT2 Reading and AT3 Writing. It is a shorthand way of dividing up the skills and areas of work. Although some ATs are taught and tested separately, for most of the day all the ATs are combined in the classroom. A teacher of English may talk with the pupils about a topic (Listening), the pupils may then study a chapter in a book (Reading), discuss it in class (Speaking) and produce an essay for homework (Writing).

How well pupils are doing is defined by *Attainment Levels*, which start at Level 1 (what 5-year-olds will do on starting school) and rise to Level 8 for very good work achieved by older pupils. As a very general guide, the national average expectation is as follows:

| Average ability at age | Level |
|:---:|:---:|
| 7 | 2 |
| 11 | 4 |
| 14 | 5-6 |

Grades 7 and 8 may be awarded at Key Stage 3 but at 16+ the Attainment Levels are replaced by GCSE grades from A* to G.

You may now be less confused when your child comes home and tells you that he has reached Level 5 in AT1 and Level 6 in AT2.

How will pupils know what level they have reached? There are two forms of assessment: *Teacher Assessment*, which can take place at any time, and *National Tests*, sometimes known as Standard Assessment Tests (SATs), which take place in May for pupils at the end of Year 9. Parents receive the results of the

National Tests in English, Maths and Science, and of Teacher Assessments in other subjects by the end of the school year in July.

In addition to the subjects identified above, the National Curriculum identifies five *cross-curricular themes:*

- economic and industrial understanding
- careers education and guidance
- environmental education
- health education
- citizenship.

These themes are clearly important if pupils are to have a broad and balanced preparation for adult life. They have no separate place in the curriculum but are touched on in a number of the conventional subjects. Some schools put on special events, sometimes involving the local community (industry, commerce), to help pupils become more aware of the issues.

# Key Stage 3

The first three years of secondary schooling provide a general grounding in a wide range of subjects. English, Mathematics, Science, Geography, History, Physical Education, Art, Music and Religious Education will be fairly familiar to most parents from their own schooldays but the content of the subjects and the way of learning them may well be different (see Chapter 4).

A Modern Language will be on offer and many schools now give pupils a choice between French and German. Others give all pupils an introductory course in two or three languages so that they can choose the one they like best in Year 8. Having introduced the first foreign language in Year 7, some schools offer pupils the chance to take up a second language in Year 8 or in Year 9. This is a detail on which parents should seek clarification when the child starts at secondary school.

Technology is no longer restricted to woodwork for boys and cookery for girls as it was for previous generations. Indeed, all subjects must by law now be available to both sexes and the usual pattern is for pupils in Key Stage 3 to sample work with metal, wood, plastic, fabrics and food. The emphasis is on designing, problem-solving and making, rather than simply carrying out instructions to make a key-rack that matches the teacher's as closely as possible. Nevertheless, there will be practical work and you will be asked from time to time to help by providing materials or by paying a small contribution towards the purchase of materials. If this happens, the law states that you must become the owners of the product of the Technology lesson. The scones are yours to eat and enjoy!

Information Technology (IT), which, in the first National Curriculum was part of Technology, has a separate Programme of Study. In Key Stage 3 pupils will be developing their IT capability, learning how to search for information, how to collect data and how to analyse and display their findings. There may be a designated lesson for IT but in most schools there is an increasing tendency for IT also to be used across the curriculum, i.e. as a learning tool in support of various subjects. One of the difficulties faced in secondary schools is that pupils come with a wide range of experience in this subject, depending on the primary school they have attended and on their experience of computers at home.

Other subjects may also be taught in Key Stage 3 even though they are not formally required. Most schools offer Drama, which is usually built on children exploring themes and acting out their own plays rather than on producing Shakespeare. Another probable subject on the timetable will be Personal and Social Education (PSE) in which pupils cover a range of topics, for example friendship, bullying, conflict, the environment, healthy living, social rights and responsibilities.

Parents need to be aware of their own rights in relation to some sensitive areas of the curriculum:

## Sex education

All schools have to have an agreed policy on sex education. By law sex education must be made available to all pupils. Parts of this will take place in the Science Programmes of Study, but teaching about AIDS, HIV and other sexually transmitted diseases and non-biological aspects of human sexual behaviour is specifically excluded from Science. This is often covered in PSE and parents have the right to withdraw their child from such lessons if they wish. If, because of your cultural or religious beliefs, you have specific requirements for the way in which your child should receive sex education, discuss this with a teacher. The school may be able to adapt its approach to meet your needs.

Education about types of contraception and where they can be obtained may be provided to pupils (other than those who have been withdrawn from sex education by their parents). If approached by an individual pupil under 16, a teacher would be more likely to make the pupil aware of leaflets and outside agencies who can provide confidential advice and treatment. If a teacher suspects that an under-age pupil is engaging in sexual activity and is at risk, he is in a difficult position, especially if the pupil concerned has confided in him. Teachers will usually encourage pupils to share their concerns with their parents but it is not legally clear that a teacher is required to inform a parent in such circumstances.

## Religious education

Schools must provide Religious Education for all pupils. The LEA agrees a syllabus for its schools which has to take account of religions other than Christianity. However, a government circular specifies that Christianity should predominate as it is the main religious tradition of this country. Voluntary schools with a particular religious affiliation may offer Religious Education according to their trust deed (for example specifically Roman Catholic or Anglican). In GM schools the agreed syllabus can be taken from any LEA, not just the local one. Parents are permitted to withdraw their children from Religious Education but must not expect the school to provide alternative teaching. The pupil withdrawn will probably work privately in the school library.

## Collective worship

The law requires there to be an act of collective worship at some point in the school day. The nature of this activity is the responsibility of the Head in conjunction with the Governors and it is expected that the worship will be 'broadly Christian' without being linked to any particular denomination, except in the case of denominational schools. Parents are permitted to withdraw their children from collective worship without giving a reason. In some cases, schools make special provision for separate non-Christian acts of worship. In practice, very few secondary schools are able to meet the requirements of the law in full.

## Political education

This is not a formal part of the curriculum but may well appear in a number of subjects (History, Geography, Social Science) and be covered in PSE. The only specification in the law is that there should be a balanced presentation of opposing views. This is not an issue on which parents may exercise their right of withdrawal but if they have concerns on this matter, they should make them known to the Headteacher who must take the necessary steps to comply with the law.

The right of withdrawal is an important protection of the sensitivities of the individual. However, before withdrawing your child you should consider how he will feel about this: withdrawal can create a barrier between your child and his peer group.

# *Year 9: choosing the options for GCSE*

The courses in Key Stage 4 (Years 10 and 11) offer pupils an element of choice. They still have to study English, Maths, Science, a Modern Foreign Language, Technology and PE and RE (the last two not usually for an exam) but the rest of the timetable can be completed with options they have chosen.

Good schools will make every effort to inform and involve parents, usually starting early in the Spring Term of Year 9. Do not miss these opportunities of showing an interest in your children's future. Beyond attending meetings, how can you help?

- By taking an interest, offering advice but not seeking to interfere. This is not easy when young people may be at the stage of rejecting most things a parent says!
- By helping them find out all the information they may need about how their choices may affect future careers.
- By understanding that there are conflicting pressures on young people as they make choices:
  - pressure from other pupils who want to keep together in doing their favourite subjects
  - pressure from parents and even grandparents who push their children to make the choices they wish they had made when they were young
  - pressure even from teachers who want to recruit to their particular subject.
- By recognising that the world into which your children are growing is different from the one you have known:
  - they will probably not stay in one job all through their lives but will move around, not only within this country but possibly within Europe and even further afield, far more readily than you did
  - they will need to be flexible, i.e. they need to be good at

    learning new skills, not set in their ways, and to relate easily to other people and be good at communicating.

- By not depressing your children's aspirations by telling them that they are being over-ambitious, yet, at the same time, by being realistic about their abilities and long-term prospects.
- By encouraging your children to choose the subject and not the teacher. Too often young people are attracted to a subject because they like the particular teacher, only to find that the teacher has been given a different group to teach in the following September, or has even left the school.

You should be able to get a lot of information from school to help you. Many schools now have a good data-bank of information and test-scores on pupils and should be able to give you a realistic assessment of what he is likely to achieve at GCSE and even beyond. The Careers and Guidance service will provide all the information you need to match qualifications to possible careers.

Be prepared for the possibility that the ideal combination of subjects for your child may not be possible in the school because of timetabling constraints. In these days when schools are short of money, it may not be possible to run a group if too few pupils opt for it. You may want to negotiate this with the Deputy Head or other senior teacher responsible for the curriculum but it may not be possible to meet all requests. Make sure that the second or third choice subjects are ones that your child wants to do.

Some of the subjects which require particular thought are:

## Science

Most schools offer Double Science which means that pupils spend 20 per cent of the week studying a mixture of Biology, Chemistry and Physics, possibly with some Geology or Astronomy. This counts as two subjects at GCSE. It is also possible to take Single Science which means spending 8 to 10 per cent of the week studying the same mixture as with Double Science but in less depth. It does not mean that you can take just one science subject. Single Science may appeal to those who are weak at Science or who are already sure that they will not want to take Science beyond 16+ and can therefore concentrate on other subjects. Some schools, mainly in the independent sector, offer the three separate sciences of Biology, Physics and Chemistry. This has the advantage of pushing the pupils well along the science track but reduces the number of other subjects they can take. All Science pathways are kept open by taking a Double Science course.

## Modern Languages

All pupils, other than those disapplied from (i.e. permitted not to follow) the National Curriculum because of learning difficulties, continue with foreign language study at Key Stage 4, and it is possible to study this as a Short Course, i.e. for half the time required for the full GCSE. The exam will be at the same standard even if the content is less extensive and this is therefore not an easy option. Many schools offer pupils the chance to continue with both their foreign languages but this is becoming increasingly rare because it limits the other options available. It is important to remember that it is difficult to pick up a language again later in the Sixth Form if it has been dropped at the end of Year 9.

## The Expressive Arts

As well as offering conventional Music and Drama, schools are now developing courses which combine these with, say, Dance and Art. Most schools recommend that all pupils should take an expressive arts subject in order to have a balanced timetable.

## Technology

It is no longer crucial to think in terms of choosing a particular technology course with a view to a long-term career. Resistant materials, Graphic products, Textiles and Food are all essentially about problem-solving, research, development and evaluation and less about the development of highly specific and technical skills. In some schools Technology is offered as a Short Course linked to another subject such as Business Studies, though this option is less likely to give an adequate foundation for Advanced Level courses.

## Humanities

Although Geography and History are not compulsory in Key Stage 4, most schools recommend that all pupils should continue with at least one of these two subjects, but might offer alternatives such as Social Science or Combined Humanities. These subjects are also available as Short Courses and advice should be sought from subject teachers as to whether a Short Course is an adequate basis for further study beyond 16.

## New subjects

Many schools give pupils the chance to start a subject they may not have done in Key Stage 3. Social Science, Business Studies, Psychology, Child Development, Geology and Physical Education for GCSE are just a few examples. These may offer a novelty attraction for a pupil but you need to find out what skills are required and what openings they may lead to in later life.

## New vocational courses

Schools are now beginning to offer 14-year-olds a vocational course, usually in place of two GCSE subjects. These include Manufacturing, Art and Design, and Leisure and Tourism. Although these courses cover general knowledge about the world of work, they do not aim to train for a specific job. In the past schools steered pupils into these courses because they were unlikely to do well in GCSE exams, but the new Part One General National Vocational Qualification (GNVQ) is intended for pupils of all abilities. It is likely that most schools will include vocational options in their Key Stage 4 curriculum. Pupils who do not take the whole Part One GNVQ may gain unit accreditation towards further study.

# Key Stage 4: getting through to GCSE

Having chosen the right subjects, your child will now have to settle down to the hard work of studying for the General Certificate of Secondary Education (GCSE), the national exam taken at the end of Year 11. This exam is graded from A* down to G, with a U being an unclassified score. The higher grades A* to C are usually regarded as 'good grades' and many Sixth Forms or other colleges will specify the number of these grades to be achieved for entry to their courses.

Here are some of the recent developments of which you need to be aware:

## Work experience

Part of the Key Stage 4 curriculum is the chance to do a week or maybe two weeks of experience in a place of work. This is an excellent opportunity for the development of maturity and worth giving your fullest support, even though you may initially worry about the loss of two weeks' preparation for GCSE. You may even be able to help your school by suggesting places where pupils could be placed, though it is not thought to be a good idea for your child to come and work in the same place as you. One of the advantages of work experience is that it requires young people to relate to adults in a new environment.

## Records of Achievement

Instead of termly or annual school reports of the kind you remember ('Could do better'), schools now use a Record of Achievement folder in which subject reports are entered, including comments by the pupils themselves on their own progress, and a record of all their other extra-curricular achievements. Encourage your children to take this seriously as it is a good framework in which they can evaluate their own progress and set targets. A good Record of Achievement folder often helps with job and college applications later on.

## Tiered exam papers

Although the GCSE is a single examination system covering the whole ability range, in many subjects there are two or three tiers of papers. Each tier has a restricted number of grades. The Foundation tier usually allows candidates to achieve grades C to G; the Intermediate tier is for grades B to F; the Higher tier is for candidates likely to get A* to C. The choice of tier is an important one and something your child's school will take seriously. If they place her in too low a tier, she may not get the grade she is capable of; if they place her in too high a tier, she may get no grade at all. The tiering of the entry will probably be related to the school's 'setting' system for each subject. If you are unclear about what this means for your own child, ask the Head of Year, Head of Department or Deputy Head for an explanation.

## Coursework

In many subjects your child will be required to do coursework as part of the exam. This will not normally count for more than 20 per cent of the marks available but it will need careful attention and planning. You must not, of course, do your child's coursework for him but you can help him by:

- suggesting ideas, sources of information and by putting him in touch with people who can throw an interesting light on the subject
- commenting on the draft of the coursework in a constructive way

- suggesting he use a dictionary where spelling seems to be a problem
- finding out the deadlines for handing in the work so as to avoid a last-minute panic
- preventing the coursework from becoming such an obsession that it interferes with homework in other subjects.

## Mock exams

Your child will probably take mock exams at the end of the first term of Year 11 or shortly after Christmas. This is a good opportunity for improving exam technique, so encourage him to approach these mocks seriously. The results need to be interpreted carefully to avoid either despair (if they were disappointing) or complacency (if they seemed quite good). The important issues to reflect on are:

- Did he time the exam correctly, i.e. did he leave enough time to check the work, and not write too briefly nor finish too early?
- What gaps in his knowledge did the exam reveal? He must concentrate on these over the next few months.

## Sitting the exams

The GCSE exams themselves start shortly after the Easter holidays with practical and oral exams. Even though pupils know this, it always seems to come as a shock. Planning the revision period needs careful thought (see Chapter 4). As a generalisation, girls are well-organised and yet get depressed because they are not working hard enough; boys leave it all far too late, pretend to be rather blasé about the whole business and think they can bluff their way through on the day.

Good personal organisation during the GCSE exams is essential. Surprising though it may seem, there are some pupils every year who turn up on the wrong day or at the wrong time, or forget to bring a vital piece of equipment. The school will emphasise the importance of this, but it is a good idea to have a copy of the exam timetable clearly displayed at home.

## Trips out of school

During Years 10 and 11 there are often opportunities for field study trips, foreign exchanges and social outings, as well as the work experience fortnight already mentioned. Excellent though these are, they amount to a significant reduction in the actual classroom time available. Without discouraging your children from taking part, it is important to keep an eye on the balance and, above all, to make sure that they catch up with work missed while they have been out of school.

# Education beyond 16: making the right choice

Nearly 80 per cent of young people now stay on in some kind of education after the age of 16. The days of leaving school and going straight into a job appear to have gone for the vast majority, probably forever.

The key questions you will have to think about with your sons and daughters are these:

- Should they stay on in education, should they pursue one of the training options described below or should they try to find a job, at least for a while?
- If the school has a Sixth Form, should they stay on in the same school or move to another school, or a Sixth Form College or a College of Further Education?
- What subjects or course should they choose?

# Leaving full-time education

For those who decide that they wish to leave full-time education at this point, there are a number of options, including:

## The Youth Credit scheme

This is a work-related training option through which young people can gain practical experience of work and at the same time gain qualifications such as NVQs (National Vocational Qualifications). These are skills-based training programmes for specific vocational areas, such as secretarial or bricklaying – in fact almost any job. Training credits up to the value of £2,500 are given to each person to buy training up to NVQ Level 2. These can be used for up to three years after leaving school. The training must be provided by training organisations approved by the local Training and Enterprise Council (TEC).

## Modern apprenticeships

These are for 16- and 17-year-olds who, ideally although not necessarily, are given employee status. Youth Credits can be used towards the costs of training which must be to at least NVQ Level 3.

## Staying on: choosing a course

You can support your child by guiding but not hustling her through the decision-making process. All the issues referred to in connection with Year 9 options are relevant here too, except that the significance of the choices to be made is greater. You can help by giving her the opportunity to talk with people in various fields of work and by keeping up to date on how the worlds of industry, commerce and the traditional professions are changing. Try to resist the temptation to direct her to the career path you have followed yourself (or would like to have followed).

During Year 11, probably shortly after the mock results have become available, the school will offer guidance evenings when you will be able to hear about the courses which are available locally. Your child will have had guidance from the Careers Service and will have had the chance to hear about the best courses leading to specific careers in which she is interested.

The range of courses available gets broader every year. It is now widely recognised that a division between specialist academic subjects (three Advanced Levels) and vocational subjects tradition-ally taught in FE Colleges is out-dated and irrelevant to the world into which we are moving. A new qualifications framework for 16-to 19-year-olds has been devised by Sir Ron Dearing and will probably be in place from September 1998.

The options available will probably be:

## Advanced Level

This will be achieved by:

- taking courses at Advanced and Advanced Subsidiary Level. It is possible that students will take 5 AS Levels in Year 12 and then narrow down to 3 in Year 13
- taking a course at the Advanced Level of GNVQ (equivalent to two A Levels)
- achieving Level 3 of a National Vocational Qualification (NVQ).

## Intermediate Level

This will be achieved by:

- obtaining GCSE grades A* to C
- taking a course at GNVQ Intermediate Level (equivalent to four higher grade GCSEs)
- achieving an NVQ at Level 2.

In addition, all students beyond 16, regardless of their course of study, should develop the following key skills:

- communication
- application of number
- information technology.

An AS Level in Key Skills is envisaged as a fundamental new qualification, and Key Skills will continue to form a part of vocational qualifications, as well as being incorporated into other A and AS Levels as appropriate.

Matching your child's likely achievements at GCSE with an appropriate post-16 course is something on which you, your child and the school have to work closely. You will need to study the information the school provides in detail.

## Staying on: where to study

The option of staying on in the same school or moving to college is not available to everyone. It depends on where you live. In some areas the nearest college is too far away; in other areas all schools stop at 16 and a change of establishment is inevitable; in yet others, there is a genuine choice. What factors should guide that choice?

The move to a College of Further Education or Sixth Form College offers:

- the chance to make a fresh start
- the opportunity of making new friends
- the possibility of taking a wider combination of courses than a school with a small Sixth Form can offer
- a more adult environment where there may well be a substantial number of older learners mixing with 17-year-olds.

Staying on in the Sixth Form of the same school has these advantages:

- there is a smooth transition from Year 11 to Year 12

- no time is wasted in settling down as your child already knows most of his fellow students and the teachers
- your child will be given the opportunity to exercise leadership – for example by being elected to the school council (see Chapter 5) – or may have the chance to assist with the learning programmes of younger pupils and this will have a maturing influence on him
- you as a parent know most of the staff already and know who to turn to if help is needed.

Whatever course of action your child eventually settles on, you need to be aware of the entry requirements. A course which involves A and AS Levels will almost certainly require at least five higher grade GCSEs and probably a B or even an A in the subjects chosen. The entry requirement for Advanced GNVQ may be slightly lower but not much. If your child already has an idea of what course of study he might like to take at university, consult the Careers department so that you and he are sure that he has the right combination of subjects to gain entry. There are specialised books available for you to consult and these are updated each year.

## Making the most of the opportunity

Although as a parent you may think that your influence over your now grown-up children is diminishing, they still need your support and interest. You need, for example, to be aware that it is not uncommon for students to take a while to settle into the new routine of Sixth Form or college work.

The biggest difference is that they will have some free time during the working day when they are expected to organise their own work schedule and do private study. This comes as a big challenge for many who have been used to having their work carefully structured for them in Key Stages 3 and 4 and expect to be told explicitly what work has to be done. It can be difficult for less mature students to learn to use their time effectively.

Your child needs to plan her working week carefully so that she can combine study, an increasing social or sporting life and possibly a part-time job. Even though your daughter may now feel independent, she is still under your responsibility. It will be helpful to her if you can continue to take an interest in her work, even though she may by now have long outstripped your own personal knowledge of her specialist subjects.

An important change in the pattern of post-16 work is that many subjects are now structured as *modular exams.* Instead of the whole two years' work being examined in a big bang at the end, the work is examined at two, three or even four points during the course. This means that a gentle or rather casual first year in the Sixth Form is no longer a good idea. Modular exams release one pressure, that of being in poor health or tensed up during the final exam, and replace it with another pressure, the need to keep up consistent effort all through the course.

The same issues that we raised in connection with planning work for GCSE, such as awareness of deadlines for handing in coursework, apply even more so at A and AS Level.

In spite of all this emphasis on work and study, life in a Sixth Form or in a college offers many other opportunities which should not be missed. Perhaps the most valuable are those chances to be involved in the running of the school or college, by supporting younger pupils by listening to them read or running clubs for them, by serving on councils or committees, or by taking the lead in promoting extra-curricular activities and community service outside school. Encourage your son or daughter to seek out opportunities for developing their organisational skills, their gifts as a public speaker, their talents as actors or musicians. These may well have long-term benefits as influential as the accumulation of good exam grades.

During the first term of Year 13, the process of applying to university, college or for work will be starting. After coming successfully through the gates of Years 9 and 10, and Years 11 and 12, you will by now be an expert in helping to gather information, take advice, reflect dispassionately, and plan ahead. The difference this time is that your son or daughter really will have to exercise much more initiative in looking at the options beyond 18.

A detailed consideration of the university entry process is beyond the scope of this book but there will be plenty of help available from the Careers department in your child's school. Every university produces a detailed handbook and you will find a list of other books and useful organisations at the end of this chapter. Bear in mind that students can now complete part of their course at a University in another European country. Some university courses encourage or require European work experience and one of the good uses of a year between school and university is to spend time working in another European country.

If, when the examination results are published in August, your son or daughter achieves what is needed for the next stage in his or her career, you can justifiably feel that you have contributed to their success by helping to guide them during the long journey through secondary education. But remember, it is they who have achieved it, not you!

## *Further reading*

**Decisions at 15/16+,** M. Smith, V. Matthew, Hobsons.

**Further choice and quality: the Charter for Further Education,** the Department for Education and Employment, a guide written for parents.

**GNVQ: is it for you?** S. Straw, Hobsons.

**Higher quality and choice: the Charter for Higher Education,** the Department for Education and Employment, another guide for parents.

**How to choose your A levels,** J.D.G. Noel and S.N. Cohen (eds), Trotman.

**How to choose your GCSEs,** Alan Vincent, Trotman.

**It's your choice – a guide to choosing the next steps at 16+,** Department for Education and Employment.

**Our children's education: the updated Parents Charter,** Department for Education and Employment.

**A parent's guide to the National Curriculum,** Ted Wragg, Nelson/WH Smith, ISBN 0 17 401310 8. This is a concise but useful summary of the National Curriculum from 5 to 16.

**13+: Pathways to success,** Karen Gold, Hobsons/CRAC (Careers Research Advisory Council), ISBN 1 86017 151 6. This is an excellent guide to choices for GCSE and beyond.

**Student grants and loans,** a brief guide for higher education students, is published by the Department for Education and Employment.

**Which way now?** Department for Education and Employment in conjunction with BBC Radio 1.

**Your choice of A levels,** Hobsons.

# Useful organisations

## Information on exams and other qualifications

**BTEC (Business and Technician Education Council),** Central House, Upper Woburn Place, London WC1H 0HH. Tel: 0171 413 8400.

**City and Guilds,** 1 Giltspur Street, London EC1A 9DD. Tel: 0171 278 2468.

**Department for Education and Employment (DfEE),** Sanctuary Buildings, Great Smith Street, London SW1P 3BT. Tel: 0171 925 6474. Publications Department: PO Box 2193, London E15 2EU. Tel: 0181 533 2000.

**RSA Examinations Board,** Progress House, Westwood Way, Coventry CV4 8HS. Tel: 01203 470033.

## Publishers

**Hobsons** Publishers of a wide range of books on choices of course and career. Tel: 01403 710851.

**Trotman** is another publisher active in this area. Tel: 0181 332 2132.

## Europe

If you are interested in studying or working in Europe, contact:

**Eurodesk,** Central Bureau, Seymour Mews, London W1U 9PE. Tel: 0171 486 5101

**Eurodesk,** 5th Floor, Ty Nant, 180 High Street, Swansea SA1 5AP. Tel: 01792 457 456.

## University admissions

Information on the university admissions system can be obtained from:

**The Universities and Colleges Admissions Service (UCAS),** Fulton House, Jessop Avenue, Cheltenham, Glos. GL50 3SH. Tel: 0242 222444.

## Sex education

If you are concerned about the place of sex education in the curriculum, contact:

**Sex Education Forum,** 8 Wakley Street, London EC1V 7QE. Tel: 0171 843 6051/2.

# CHAPTER FOUR

# Helping children to learn more effectively

The aim of this chapter is to help you to enable your children to learn more effectively, whatever their ability. By understanding how young people are taught and how they learn, you will be able to encourage them to make better progress. Although many parents feel daunted by the difficulty of the subject content at secondary level, ('they didn't do that in Chemistry when I was at school'), parents who know how to help can make a tremendous difference.

In this chapter we will be looking at:

- how pupils are taught in secondary schools
- how pupils learn
- homework and study skills
- revising for examinations
- the different learning patterns of boys and girls
- achievement of children from ethnic minorities
- very able children
- children with special educational needs
- enhancing children's learning and increasing self-esteem.

# How pupils are taught in secondary schools

The biggest difference between the way you were probably taught at school a generation ago and what your children experience today can be summed up in the word *variety*. You probably spent most of your time listening (or not, as the case may be) to a teacher standing at the front of a whole class. You would take notes from what was being said, sometimes copying them from the blackboard and then learn them for homework. The next day you would be tested on your ability to recall what you had done in previous lessons. Alongside this you would work your way systematically through a text book in most subjects, reading, learning, summarising and doing exercises and problems for homework. There was practical work, of course, but it was mainly confined to carrying out experiments or completing manual tasks previously demonstrated by the teacher.

In many schools there were exceptional teachers who did not conform to that stereotype and more progressive methods were gradually introduced into the secondary sector, but rather later than in primary schools. The pattern of teaching in secondary schools today is much more varied. As well as the formal, traditional style of whole-class teaching described above (to which some politicians advocate a return), pupils are taught in different groupings, using varied media and carrying out a range of activities. Lessons still usually last about an hour.

## Grouping

In many subjects pupils work in groups for part or the whole of the lesson. After an initial presentation by the teacher, a group of pupils working together tackle a problem, act out a role play, or debate an issue in order to report back their findings to the whole class. Sometimes the groupings are based on friendships, i.e.

pupils choose who they want to work with. Sometimes they are based on ability, i.e. pupils are grouped so that those pupils of similar ability work together. For some activities teachers may specifically create groups of mixed ability and may sometimes group by gender. In some subjects pupils work in pairs, for example in modern languages, to develop oral skills. In other subjects they work as individuals, for example in design subjects or on the computer. Sometimes, when they work as a whole class, they may sit in a circle in order to engage more effectively in discussion.

Schools operate varying combinations of mixed-ability grouping, setting, banding, and streaming. In a **mixed-ability class** will be pupils from the entire ability range in the school but if the school has a selected entry, this means that the ability level of the members of the group will be fairly similar. **Streaming** is the system by which, within a school, children are grouped by general ability and taught as a whole group for several subjects. If the main factor in deciding the streaming is, say, English language, a pupil with poor mathematical skills in a top stream might find the work difficult. It is more common to use **setting**, where pupils are grouped for each subject according to their ability in that specific subject. This is easier to achieve in larger secondary schools where there is greater timetabling flexibility. **Banding** is a system whereby the year group is divided into broad bands of ability, for example an upper band and lower band. They may then be setted or streamed within the band.

Very few comprehensive schools now use mixed-ability grouping right through from Year 7 to 11. The most common pattern is for a mixed-ability Year 7 with setting introduced progressively through subsequent years.

## Teaching materials and methods

Today's teachers have a wide range of media at their disposal. Pupils learn not only from text books but by watching schools television programmes, by using computer programs, by filling in work sheets (sometimes produced by the teacher), by using a wide range of materials in Design, by acting (not only in Drama), by listening to tapes played to a whole class or individualised on headsets. Teachers aim to make the lessons as varied and demanding as possible, often using a number of different teaching techniques within the same lesson.

## Developing skills

Alongside the basic and traditional aim of imparting knowledge, today's teachers are seeking to develop a wide range of skills and abilities:

- the ability to solve problems
- the skills of oral communication and debate
- the skills of written communication (there is now a renewed emphasis on spelling accuracy)
- the ability to analyse arguments and challenge conclusions
- the ability to empathise (to understand how another person feels)
- the ability to use technology to seek out relevant information
- the skill of working collaboratively with others
- the skill of learning how to learn.

This broader definition of the teaching process needs to be understood by parents so that they can better appreciate the kind of work their children will be bringing home to do or will talk about in answer to the age-old question 'What did you do at school today?' If the answer from your child is 'nothing', it may be that it is all so complicated to explain that he does not know where to start.

What teachers are aiming to do is to equip pupils not only with the basic knowledge they will require for the future but above all with the range of skills and flexibility which tomorrow's world will demand.

# How pupils learn

Young people learn in a variety of ways:

- They learn factual information which they commit to memory so that they can recall it quickly if they need it: *When did the First World War start?*
- They learn to understand and explain: *Why do we feel cold when our skin is wet?*
- They learn to imagine and create, expressing themselves in writing, in music or in art form: *Write a poem about a rain storm. Write a piece of music to represent rain falling. Paint a picture of a landscape after heavy rain.*
- They learn to apply knowledge and to use processes to arrive at answers: *If x = 2 and y = 3, what is the value of 4x + 2y?*
- They learn to analyse information, evidence and data, to arrive at conclusions based on the evidence and then to express their thoughts in an orderly fashion: *What evidence would you use to disprove Darwin's theories of the evolution of man?*
- They learn to synthesise, i.e. bring together their knowledge, their understanding and their imagination to tackle demanding problems: *What do you suppose people would do if the world ran out of natural fuels like coal and oil?*
- They learn to evaluate, bringing together knowledge and opinions to make value judgements which they have to justify with rational argument: *Is it true that advertising has a great effect on public opinion and what are the implications for democratic freedom?*

Parents need to realise that young people learn through reading, listening, observing, measuring, discussing, doing and by communicating with others. Encourage your child to develop as broadly as possible and not to neglect any aspect of learning.

You can do this by encouraging your child to keep on reading from a wide variety of sources: fiction, history, biography, poetry, drama, newspapers, magazines. Encourage him to talk about what he has been reading and to challenge the ideas that have been put before him. Encourage him to explore his particular fields of interest – visiting castles, collecting fossils, training an animal, playing an instrument – so that he can develop the skills outlined above in an area which captivates him. Very few children can be interested in everything and you may feel frustrated when your children develop specialised interests which you do not share. It is part of the fascination of parenthood when a son or daughter becomes an expert and can then teach his or her own parents!

All this may sound very theoretical and idealistic so let's come down to earth and look at how you can help.

# *Homework and study skills*

Homework is a thorny problem for all of us. It was originally devised as a way of keeping boys out of mischief in the gap between supper and bed-time in 19th century boarding schools and was adopted by state grammar schools in the 1920s as a way of raising academic standards to those of the public schools.

It is resented by some young people as an intrusion by teachers on their private time: 'Why should we have to do overtime?' It is resented by some parents because it is a daily battleground within the family. It is resented by some teachers because it brings a massive workload of marking in some subjects like English, History and Geography.

Like it or not, homework is here to stay and there is even talk of making it more tightly defined by government decree, so we have to learn how to make the best of it. There is evidence that homework makes a difference and that children who do regularly marked homework do better at school than those who do not, even allowing for differences in home background.

Well managed homework can pay off in a number of ways:

- it helps children learn and practise the basic skills of reading, writing and maths
- it gives them a chance to learn, remember and understand facts
- it gives them a chance to look at new ideas and find new information by using a library, or by talking to people who know something about, say, the project they are working on
- it helps them learn how to plan, set goals and manage time
- at best it helps them to develop a positive attitude towards lifelong and self-directed learning.

Parents can help in many practical ways:

## Creating a space

Children work best at home when they have a clear space on which to lay out their books and where they can be quiet, if they want to be. Many parents are anxious because their children try to do homework with distracting music in the background, but some people do find it easier to work in that way. Doing homework while watching television should be firmly discouraged. If the working space provided is shared with others, make sure that other members of the family respect it. Ready access to paper, pencils, dictionary, calculator, thesaurus, and a one-volume encyclopaedia helps to make it easier to start. It is often getting started that is the most difficult part of the process.

## Helping with time management

There is no best time for homework. Some like to get it done straight away on arriving home; others prefer to have a little break first and may have other family responsibilities such as looking after a younger sibling; others prefer to do homework immediately after a meal. You can help your children work out what is the best time for them and then encourage them to get into good habits of personal discipline and organisation. Time management also extends to planning the work over the week so that other valuable activities – evening clubs, music practice, scouts, guides – are not squeezed out. Most schools advise teachers not to set homework to be handed in on the following day.

The question parents often ask is: how much time should my child be spending on homework? Attempts to specify the exact length of time are made by some schools and even by some politicians but in reality a lot depends on the ability and attitude of the individual pupil. In secondary school, 60 to 90 minutes per evening would be typical in Key Stage 3, rising to two hours in Key Stage 4, with a further two to four hours at the weekend. If your child does not have enough work to do to fill the time set aside for homework, encourage her to read, or to review work done earlier.

## *Guiding not doing*

Show an interest in what your children are doing but do not do it for them. Help them to understand what it is they are supposed to do and make sure they have the equipment they need. Be cautious about trying to call on your rusty knowledge to explain how things were done when you were at school. Be available to help with routine testing of memorised material (French vocabulary, scientific formulae, historical and geographical data), bearing in mind what was said earlier about this being much less of a feature of learning than it used to be.

## *Using technology*

Many parents raised in the pre-computer age worry about whether or not they should buy a computer for home use. We have to recognise that

- we live in an information age dominated by computers
- increasingly, the workplace expects us to be familiar with computers

- our future workforce must be IT literate in order to be successful
- although IT skills are taught in school, pupils with access to computers at home have an advantage
- most young people prefer playing computer games to using it as a tool for learning.

If you can afford one, a computer at home is, on balance, an asset provided it is used appropriately. Presenting work in word-processed form encourages your child to revise and redraft, to aim for high standards and rehearses the very marketable skills of word-processing. The appeal of a computer to boys may be enough to encourage them to do more work. Girls, who are typically less attracted by computers, may be persuaded when they realise that it can produce better and neater results, a feature of work in which girls like to excel. You must remember that the merit of a computer is that it can be used for word-processing, desk-top publishing, graphics, databases and spreadsheets. As a vehicle for playing sophisticated computer games, it is of questionable value.

Which computer to buy? The school may be able to advise you or you may choose the same one as you are familiar with at work. It does not matter if the computer you have at home is different to the one your child uses at school: the different technologies are converging rather than diverging and any experience in using software packages is helpful for learning to use others in future. Access to multi-media encyclopaedias on CD-ROM is also valuable. The Oxford English Dictionary on CD-ROM is a huge enhancement of the printed version.

Consider placing a home computer in a public area of the home. This makes supervision easier and for Internet use in particular, it helps to avoid the private obsessions which can take place in a bedroom. It also enables the whole family to share and discuss its use.

What should your attitude be towards taking material direct

HELPING CHILDREN TO LEARN MORE EFFECTIVELY

from a CD-ROM or from the Internet, perhaps to do a project or a piece of coursework? Living as we do in an 'information age', the skills of searching for and using information are vital for tomorrow's adults. However, there is a distinction to be made between positive information handling and mindless copying.

Before the invention of computers, pupils tended not to crib extensive passages from printed books because copying it all out was too much like hard work. When it did happen, it was always obvious to the teacher because the style would be different from what the pupil normally wrote. Taking information from the Internet or from an encyclopaedia on a CD-ROM is not wrong provided that the pupil has made a personal input to the process: he has selected and simplified the relevant material, added a personal comment, changed the level of language to make it fit the context of the project he is working on and, where he has used a direct quotation, has acknowledged that in his footnotes. Using computerised help in this way is a perfectly valid and useful way of working.

Much will depend on the way the teacher has set the task. A project to 'write about Victorian times' is an invitation to lift passages from other sources undigested. A better task would be to 'write a day's entry in the diary of a Victorian child, describing what you see and do as you go about your day, at home, in the streets and at school'.

In his book *Information problem-solving*, Mike Eisenberg has suggested the Big Six stages for a piece of work:

1 **What do I want to know?** – define the task and identify the information needed to solve it.
2 **Information seeking strategies** – brainstorm all possible sources and select the best ones.
3 **Location and access** – find the sources.
4 **Use of information** – read or view the sources, extract the *relevant* information.
5 **Organisation and presentation** – place the information in a

coherent order with an appropriate layout and emphasis of key points.

6 **Evaluation** – was the process efficient? (Did it take longer than it needed to?) And effective? (Did it meet the criteria for the project?) How could I improve next time?

The most important point is that information should not go simply from the Internet or from any other source to the teacher without having passed actively through the mind of the pupil.

## Monitoring

Not all pupils adapt easily to the routine of regular homework and it is wise for you to keep an eye on how much time your child is devoting to it. Most schools now have a homework diary in which pupils write down what has to be done and parents can initial the page or send messages back, for example if a piece of work has taken an unreasonably long time. Make use of any guidance or opportunities offered by the school. Many now run homework clubs during the lunch-hour or after school so that pupils who do not have ideal facilities at home can work quietly and with access to the equipment they need.

It is unwise to compare the length of time taken for each subject, as the nature of the tasks set will vary. In some subjects, such as Modern Languages, there will probably be systematic learning homework every week. In other subjects, perhaps Geography or History, there may be several homeworks of reading or research before a more substantial piece of written work is expected. It is the way children use their time that matters rather than the amount of time they spend – quality rather than quantity.

## Keeping a sense of proportion

In this section we may appear to have laboured the part that you can play in supporting your children's work at home. Parents also have to help the over-assiduous child keep a sense of proportion.

Other activities matter: spending time with the family and with friends, visiting places, taking part in clubs or groups, possibly doing a part-time job, taking part in community service – all these are important things which enrich the life of a young person growing up through their teens and must not be neglected.

# Revising for examinations

Taking exams has always been a trying experience which very few people actually enjoy but in the last few years, the public scrutiny of examination results has greatly increased the pressure on schools to do well and, consequently, on pupils to achieve their best.

If the good learning habits outlined in the previous section have been well established in Years 7 and 8, the extra pressure of the GCSE period will be manageable. It is however very difficult for a child who has been casual about work habits to switch suddenly into a different mode of behaviour just weeks before an exam takes place.

Parents can help and, sometimes, well-meaning parents can hinder!

## Practical tips for parents

- Do not get in the way. Avoid hovering anxiously.
- Be available if needed (for example to test memorised material) but do not give amateur advice and do not try to get them to do Maths the way you did.
- Provide a stable and calm environment, with healthy food and drink.
- Be prepared for irritability and signs of stress, to which you respond sympathetically but without overreacting.
- Do not use bribes, blackmail or threats.

- Do not make comparisons with the way older brothers and sisters prepared for their exams.
- Do not abandon normal family activities (holidays, outings, etc.). The rest of the world has to go on living during this revision period which must be kept in perspective.

## Practical tips to pass on to pupils

- Work when you are feeling at your best, not when you have come in from a late-night party, or if you are feeling hungry.
- Plan a timetable for your revision programme and stick to it for at least a week or two. Then change it if you find that it is not going as smoothly as you had hoped. Remember to plan in some leisure as well and do not feel guilty about not working.
- Most students revise more effectively in shortish bursts of, say, 40 minutes to an hour, rather than by slogging away for several hours at a time. When you finish a revision session, make a note about what you need to do next so that you can get off to a focused start on the next occasion.
- Revise actively, i.e. by writing as well as reading. Write summaries of what you have been revising, with clear headings and key words, preferably on cards which you can use again just before the exam to trigger your memory. Do some test questions against the clock so you can improve the way you time your answering of questions.
- Consider doing your revision in varied formats. You may like to work with a friend sometimes, testing each other

and explaining to each other what you have done. Don't let it become a moaning session, a social event or an opportunity for 'psyching out'. Don't be too competitive about it: you are trying to help both of you to do better, not one to triumph. Use a variety of media, including books, tapes and videos from the local library or your school's resource centre.

- Balance work with leisure. Try to stick to a timetable with hard work first, followed by leisure for pleasure.

## Study guides

Many publishers now produce study guides and these can be a useful supplement, provided your child realises that they cannot work miracles by making up for years of idleness.

Choose with care and do not allow yourself to be conned into spending a lot of money in the mistaken belief that it is the least you can do to help out. Make sure that the study guide you are considering is up to date and not simply an old version with a sticker on the front. Is it preparing your child for the kind of examination questions she is going to face? Has it got self-correcting exercises so that she can do some questions under examination conditions? Look at the writers of the guide – are they examiners and/or practising teachers? Ask the teacher's opinion. Ask your friends about study guides their children have used in the past – a user's recommendation is worth more than an impressive book cover and a publisher's blurb. Involve your son or daughter in the selection so that they have some commitment to making it work for them.

Buying a study guide on CD-ROM does not make it any more useful if it has been badly written in the first place so don't be lured into spending more money than you need to just because it looks modern. In the long run, there is no substitute for hard work.

# The different learning patterns of boys and girls

In this section, we focus on the different ways in which boys and girls learn and what parents can do to ensure that their children achieve the best they are capable of and have access to the widest range of career opportunities. Inevitably, a discussion of these issues has to talk in terms of generalities and it may well be that your own child is an exception to the stereotype.

In recent years there has been growing awareness and concern about the apparent under-achievement of boys in public examinations. At first sight this concern could be interpreted as an insult to girls who have been improving their academic performance. Equal Opportunities policies over the last twenty years have rightly improved educational chances and access for girls but there is still a long way to go. The 'glass ceiling', which prevents women from reaching the highest positions in society, commerce, industry and government, is still a challenge for a country which claims to want to rid itself of discrimination.

It is the decline in boys' performance which has grabbed the recent headlines. Over the nation as a whole, girls out-perform boys at GCSE: 11 per cent more girls achieve five or more higher grades than boys. The difference is particularly marked in English, foreign languages and History, but even in those subjects thought to be more traditionally the male preserve – Technology, Maths and Science – girls are now overtaking boys.

It used to be said that girls mature earlier and therefore boys will eventually catch up, certainly by A Level. Even that is no longer true: girls are continuing to maintain their academic advantage at 18+ and a higher proportion of girls go on to Higher Education. It is only at the final degree level that boys appear to do better, scoring a slightly higher proportion of first-class degrees.

The reasons behind these trends are far too complex to be dealt with adequately in this book. Many of the changes in society – the decline in unskilled labouring jobs held by men, the increased proportion of jobs requiring traditionally feminine inter-personal skills, the media-promoted images of young men as boorish, beer-drinking, risk-taking, sex-obsessed louts – are beyond the control of parents faced with doing the best they can for their young sons and daughters.

## Boys

The Exeter University Survey of Young People in 1994 confirms what our day-to-day observations tell us. Looking at young people in the secondary sector, the researchers found that boys spend less time on homework, watch more television and videos and play more computer games. They read less (especially after the age of 12) and prefer to read magazines relating to their specialist interests, non-fiction books or action stories depicting macho heroes. They feel generally pleased with themselves and over-estimate their academic ability, boasting about how little work they have done. They are very aware of peer-group pressure (they must be 'one of the lads'), consider it unmanly to express feelings or to cry, and do not like to receive praise for academic success, especially in public.

## Girls

The same study depicts girls as taking academic work more seriously, spending more time on it and yet feeling uncertain about how well they have done. They have a better diet, eating more fruit and fewer chips, and they worry more about their looks, school, money, health and their career prospects. They spend less time in active physical pursuits and more time talking to their friends. They read more widely and prefer fictional works which deal with emotions and personal relations, although they also like reading books intended for boys. They are more likely to play a musical instrument, especially a violin or a flute! Although they value the approval of their friends, they are less likely to follow the gang in doing something of which they disapprove. They are less likely to be involved in illegal drugs but, paradoxically, a higher proportion smoke, though consuming fewer cigarettes per head than male smokers. Although more girls are choosing to do 'male subjects' for GCSE and A Level, gender-stereotyping is still very strong, especially in mixed schools. Girls rarely choose Physics, just as boys hardly ever choose French.

This simplified and generalised picture of young people today poses a number of important questions for schools, but what can parents do? The following list of simple suggestions is not offered as a complete and fool-proof answer but it may start you thinking.

## If you are the parent of a girl . . .

- be very positive about her ability, reassure her that she is doing well and encourage her to be assertive in class, i.e. to put her hand up to ask and answer questions
- give her every opportunity to use computer technology and assure her that she will be able to develop high level skills in information technology
- at option time (14+ and 16+), ask her to give serious consideration to the traditionally male subjects and point out the positive career prospects for women well qualified in Engineering, Physics and Natural Sciences
- approve of her good dietary habits without letting them become obsessive. Be prepared for the possibility that the stress of revising for exams might show itself in eating disorders or depression
- encourage her to take up any public speaking opportunities and school representative posts, especially in a mixed school where boys tend to volunteer more readily
- encourage her to keep up sporting activities
- let her know that you have high expectations of her, even if she does not have them of herself.

HELPING CHILDREN TO LEARN MORE EFFECTIVELY

## If you are the parent of a boy . . .

- encourage him to keep reading and to sample a wide range of books (not just science and non-fiction); offer him short-term incentives for reading. There is a list of suggested titles in Appendix 11
- try to get him to respond to the emotional content of what he reads or watches on television, i.e. to talk about what the characters were feeling, or what he felt about the situations depicted
- never say or imply that 'real men don't cry'; allow him to explore and express his feelings without embarrassment
- while giving him every encouragement in his interests in sport, outdoor pursuits and other typically masculine activities, give him the chance to try out artistic and creative pastimes
- while recognising that he will not want to stand out from the crowd, help him to exercise judgement about his peer-group's values
- do what you can to see that he takes a serious attitude towards work in the early years of secondary school and does not leave everything until the last minute
- negotiate reasonable hours of computer usage and look out for signs of addiction to computer games (the need to play every day, long periods spent alone). These are rarely of educational value
- at option time, make sure that he gives proper consideration to the whole range of subjects and does not follow the crowd into the obvious male domains. In particular, remind him that men need to be competent in foreign languages just as much as women
- when thinking about work experience and careers, remind him that men can be very effective in the caring and teaching professions and that they have an

increasing rarity value which might have financial
advantage.

The boy/girl performance dilemma raises questions of equal
opportunities and discrimination, most of which cannot be
resolved within the home. It might be a subject to suggest to the
Parents' Association as a topic for wider debate (see Chapter 6).

# *Achievement of children from ethnic minorities*

During the 1980s, much of the comment on under-achievement of
children from ethnic minorities was somewhat over-generalised. In
recent years more detailed studies have shown that there is a difference in the achievement of children from different ethnic backgrounds but the picture is quite complex. For instance,
Afro-Caribbean pupils, on average, seem to perform less well than
Asian pupils who, in some areas, perform better than white pupils.
However, there are some subjects in which each category of student performs better than another. Within the broad category of
Asian students, different average performance levels have been
found between Indian, Pakistani and Bangladeshi pupils.

What seems to be clear is that school and parental expectations
and aspirations make a great difference. It is therefore vital that
teachers and parents hold high expectations and convey them to
black and Asian children, and monitor the children's progress to
make sure they are achieving what they are capable of. Schools
must go beyond this to look at teaching methods, materials and
content, as well as the ethos of the school.

Advice for parents given elsewhere in this book about helping
children to develop a positive self-image and set appropriately
high goals for themselves is particularly relevant to children from
minority cultures who tend to under-perform within the British
educational system.

Most LEAs have developed services which provide bi-lingual support to help pupils fulfil their potential in school. Whilst under threat from funding uncertainties, such services offer valuable help for parents and children whose first language is not English.

# Very able children

If you happen to be the parent of a child with outstanding all-round ability or a particular gift, it is likely that you will be aware of this well before your child reaches secondary school age. The identification of very able children is imprecise. In some cases, test scores can give an indication that a child has very high ability, but not always. Experienced teachers carry out identification rather subjectively by spotting the child who has always finished her work early, who is keen to get back to her private reading, who asks penetrating questions and persists until she gets a satisfactory answer. A dialogue between parents and school is essential and is not always easy. Sometimes the school may feel that the parent is being over-pushy; sometimes the parent thinks the school has failed to spot her child's outstanding ability and is not responding to the child's needs.

Within the primary school setting, skilful teachers can often provide a personalised programme for a very able child which can keep him motivated and academically challenged.

You might expect there to be little problem in finding challenging work in the secondary school as the subjects become more specialised and demanding but the way a secondary school is organised can actually make it more, not less, difficult for a very able pupil. This is because most secondary schools are organised on an age-group cohort, all pupils of the same age moving forward together and following the same programme. A pupil of exceptional ability can find himself, even in a subject where there is setting by ability, working at a slow pace with children of much lesser ability or commitment. There is a serious danger of disenchantment, demotivation and even of poor behaviour if the school and the parent do not recognise the problem and work together to solve it.

## Which school?

Some parents take the view that children of very high ability work best when put together in a school with pupils of similar ability. You may therefore wish to consider applying for a place in a selective school. Some selective schools are allowed to choose pupils on the basis of particular ability, for example in Music, languages or Technology; others choose on the basis of all-round academic ability, sometimes measured by a formal entrance examination.

You may wish to send your very able child to an independent school where you might expect that she will be with some, but by no means all, pupils of similar ability. According to where you live and the quality of the state schools available, you will have to decide whether or not the cost of independent education is worth paying. Before making the final decision, think about what you could provide for your child as enrichment activity if you were to send her to a state school and use the fees you would have paid to an independent school on foreign trips, music lessons and other educational activities.

Some parents of very able children react against what they see as the divisive élitism of selective or independent schools and believe that it is important for their child to be educated alongside average and below average pupils. They nevertheless rightly feel that their child is entitled to an appropriate education.

In the very early days of the comprehensive school, there was some hostility to the concept of high ability and the need for special measures to be taken. Fortunately, the climate in secondary comprehensive schools is now completely different and most LEAs and schools have developed a policy for meeting the needs of very able children. At the time of transfer from primary to secondary school, this is certainly an issue which you should raise with the schools you are considering.

# What can schools do?

Acceleration – i.e. working with an older age-group – is one solution and is occasionally adopted. A request for early transfer from primary to secondary school should be thoroughly discussed with the primary school Head and the LEA adviser, inspector or officer. They will want to take into consideration not only your child's academic ability (is he working consistently well ahead of his peers or is this just a learning spurt?) but also his physical, social and emotional development. If they agree that early transfer is appropriate, you will need to liaise closely with the receiving secondary school, if there are spare places.

Some secondary schools offer very able pupils the possibility of acceleration in one or two subjects. In these cases, the pupil remains with his year group for the majority of the week but does Science, or Languages, or Music, with an older age-group. The feasibility of this arrangement depends on the way the school timetable is constructed and it also requires skilful handling by the subject teacher so that the older pupils do not feel undermined by the presence in their midst of a younger pupil more able than they are.

Acceleration can sometimes lead to early examination entry in one or more subjects. The implications of this need to be thought out well in advance by the school and parents working together. For example, a very able student achieving excellent A Level results at the age of 16 or 17 rather than 18 will need to plan how to spend a year productively between school and university.

Alongside or instead of acceleration, a good school will have other strategies:

- *differentiated learning material*: this means that the subject specialists devise more demanding tasks for the able children. This is easier in some subjects than others
- *withdrawal for individualised learning*: some schools have developed computer-based learning packages which very able children can work with on their own

- *mentoring by an older pupil*: schools with Sixth Forms often have schemes which enable an older pupil to be linked as a mentor to a younger pupil. Although this is most often done for children who need extra help with basic learning difficulties, there is no reason why this cannot also be done for children with high ability
- *extra-curricular activities:* a very able pupil can often work more easily at his own level in the less structured setting of an extra-curricular club. Chess, debating, music, school publications and drama can all offer a very able child a real challenge. There are also many inter-school and national competitions which provide an incentive and the kind of challenge which very able children relish
- *enrichment activity:* many schools now offer pupils with a particular talent the chance to go on weekend, holiday or evening courses which will develop their special interest. Some of these are provided free of charge by university departments, particularly during the Christmas holidays, but in other cases there will be a charge.

## What can parents do?

Above all, keep in constructive dialogue with the school. Your child has the same rights as every other child to an appropriate education. At the same time, you must recognise the financial constraints under which schools are working and the very considerable pressures upon teachers.

If your school seems short of ideas, suggest that they make contact with NACE (The National Association for Able Children in Education) who will be able to give them a lot of practical advice.

At home, you can do all the things outlined above in relation to supporting your child's learning, but to an even greater extent. You can help by enabling your child to:

- visit places of interest (castles, concerts, museums, art galleries)

- read widely as well as reading specialised magazines
- meet adults with expert knowledge in their field
- read and discuss the newspaper (not always the same one).

You may wish to consider joining the NAGC (National Association for Gifted Children) which will enable you to meet parents of children with similar abilities. You will be able to pick up some good ideas for enrichment activities and, at the same time, you will begin to realise that there are quite a lot of other children just as talented as the genius you have produced!

# Children with special educational needs

All children have individual needs – their own particular strengths, weaknesses and learning styles.

The term *special educational needs* is generally used in schools to refer to those children whose learning difficulties or disabilities are significantly greater than those of most children of that age, and who need special help in order to benefit fully from their schooling.

A child's special educational needs might arise from

- a physical impairment
- sight, hearing or speech difficulties
- learning problems – developmental (such as problems with attention, memory, perception, thinking and language) or academic (such as problems with reading, spelling, handwriting, and written expression)
- mental handicap
- emotional or behavioural problems
- a medical problem or illness.

It is estimated that about one in five children will have a special educational need at some stage of their school career. Most of these children will attend ordinary mainstream schools.

## How do I know if my child has special educational needs?

In many cases children's special educational needs become evident at primary school but problems can also emerge at the secondary school stage. You are most likely to find out that your child is experiencing problems when she tells you herself. However, some children are reluctant to discuss their difficulties – even with parents. Some may not realise the extent of their own difficulty, and put it down to lessons being 'boring'.

Your child's teachers will monitor her work and behaviour both formally and informally, and so should pick up any problems and discuss them with you.

However, if your child is new to the school, or if for any other reason the fact that she is struggling has gone unnoticed, you may become aware of the problem sooner than the school. You know your child better than the school and may spot anxiety or depression over school work. You may get a feeling that she is not able to do things as well as others of her age. National Curriculum tests may also give you some sense of her relative ability and progress.

It is vital that you bring any concerns about your child's needs and progress to the school. Good schools will respond positively and value your observations and views. The best person to contact first is usually the form tutor, who will be able to draw in other appropriate colleagues.

When a parent knows that something is wrong, it can be extremely frustrating if the school does not appear to respond. If this happens, keep talking and keep listening. Be persistent but positive in describing your concerns and in trying to understand the school's view. If the school's Special Educational Needs Coordinator (SENCO) has not been involved in the discussions you can ask for this. If you remain dissatisfied following involvement of the SENCO and then headteacher, you may want to talk to the Governor who has particular responsibility for special educational needs. This Governor will usually be named in the Governors'

Annual Report to Parents; if not, try the school office. The school's complaints procedure (see pp127–9) can also be followed.

Remember, however, that under-achievement at school can have other causes than learning difficulties, such as emotional upset, negative peer pressure, relationship problems and problems at home. Some parents have unrealistic expectations of their child and feel that there must be something wrong when they are simply performing at their own level. This may be hard to accept but be open to it as a possibility.

It is important that you use all opportunities provided by the school for consultation with teachers about your child's progress. Apart from the positive message that this gives to your child, it allows you to check that the school's views about her strengths, weaknesses and interests fit with yours. Schools are increasingly developing the way they monitor pupils' achievement against their earlier attainment, for instance, using data from diagnostic tests when pupils entered at Year 7. If your child's school uses such tests, you could ask to have the information explained to you. This can be illuminating for teachers and parents, pointing to areas of weakness, under-achievement or achievement beyond expecta-tions. However, as the school will probably warn you, there is no automatic link between the test results and future performance.

Try to follow up discussions with teachers by talking with your child about her teacher's views and suggestions. This can provide a context in which she can open up about any problems she is experiencing at school.

## What will the school do if they think my child has special educational needs?

The LEA and schools have a legal duty to identify, assess and make provision for children with special educational needs. This is the case whether your child is in an LEA or a Grant Maintained school.

The school's approach will be described in its Special

Educational Needs policy and a summary of this should be published in the school prospectus. The governing body is also required to report on how the policy has been applied in its Annual Report to Parents (see Chapter 6).

The Department for Education and Employment provides a guidance document for schools and LEAs called the *Code of Practice on the Identification and Assessment of Special Educational Needs*. All state schools must 'have regard to' the Code of Practice in the way they identify and help pupils with special educational needs.

As recommended by the Code of Practice, most schools and LEAs use a staged approach to identifying children's problems and providing special help. There is some variation across LEAs and schools, but broadly the five stages are as described in Appendix 3. Most children's special educational needs can be met at stages 1 to 3 which involve help from within the school, sometimes with advice from external agencies.

Each school is required to appoint a Special Educational Needs Co-ordinator (SENCO) who has particular responsibility for pupils at each of the stages.

At stage 3 the school can involve the LEA's Educational Psychologist in assessing your child's needs. If they don't think this is necessary, but you want an external view, you can (at your own expense) seek an assessment from an independent psychologist. However, having seen any report that an independent psychologist has produced, it will still be up to the school and the LEA to decide how to meet your child's needs. If you feel that their decisions are wrong, and you have fully explained your concerns to the school and LEA but cannot reach agreement with them, you can appeal to the SEN Tribunal (see Appendix 4 for more detail on this).

HELPING CHILDREN TO LEARN MORE EFFECTIVELY

## What sort of help will my child with special educational needs receive?

Most mainstream secondary schools have a Special Needs or Learning Support Department. It will include teachers and learning support assistants who are experienced in working with children with special educational needs.

Few schools now put children permanently into remedial classes. Pupils with special educational needs who attend mainstream schools generally spend most of their time in ordinary classes, sometimes with support from additional adults. The Learning Support Department may arrange for some pupils to be withdrawn for short periods for one-to-one or small group sessions to do more intensive work on particular areas. For example, pupils may be withdrawn for practice in basic skills (reading, writing, number work); children with emotional or behavioural difficulties may receive counselling or social skills work; children with physical impairments may have physiotherapy, hydrotherapy or other treatment.

Extra help can also take the form of specially adapted tasks or materials; special equipment; or help from a learning support assistant, a special needs teacher or a specialist/therapist from outside school. Schools often receive or buy in specialist advice and support on particular special educational needs such as behaviour problems, speech, language and literacy difficulties and sight or hearing impairment.

Over the last two decades, with greater integration of pupils with special needs into mainstream schools, teachers' experience and skills have developed. Teachers are now better at identifying problems and using a range of strategies to help children with learning difficulties. For example, they will set differentiated tasks – pitched at levels to suit children of differing abilities. The teacher's method will depend on the child's particular difficulty. For example, a pupil with Persistent Literacy Difficulties (or dyslexia) may adopt a multi-sensory approach combining visual, speaking, listening and writing tasks in a structured way, and may make greater use of computers, tape recorders and pictures than with other children.

Some mainstream schools are specially resourced, equipped, staffed or designed to provide for children with particular needs, for example, schools which are wheelchair accessible, those with speech and language units, or which have additional facilities for children with a hearing impairment.

All pupils are entitled to a broad and balanced curriculum. The vast majority of pupils with special educational needs will study the full National Curriculum. In a few cases it may be decided, after full consultation with parents, that a pupil will not study or be tested on particular aspects.

## Special schools

Some pupils have special educational needs which cannot be met in a mainstream school. This decision would be taken following a process of Statutory Assessment (described below) which involves teachers, parents and other agencies.

There are various types of day and residential special school which are resourced, equipped and staffed to meet different kinds and ranges of special educational need. For example, there are schools for children with severe or moderate learning difficulties, for children with emotional and behavioural difficulties and schools for the blind or visually impaired. Each LEA has a different make-up of special schools and there are also independent special schools which extend the range of specialist provision.

For some parents it may be a shock to learn that their child requires a special school. Many are simply relieved that their child will get specialist help in a small school setting with a high level of adult attention.

Depending on the ability of the children, some special schools operate integration arrangements with local secondary schools which provide opportunities for pupils to experience some of their lessons in the mainstream school.

As with a move to any new school, the first visit to your child's proposed special school can be enormously important in allaying fears and scotching misconceptions.

## Statutory Assessment

It is generally said that about one in 50 children across the total school population will have special needs which require Statutory Assessment. In practice, the percentage varies from one LEA to another.

Statutory Assessment is the very detailed examination of your child's problems and needs. It is called *Statutory* Assessment because the procedures are clearly laid down by law. Statutory Assessment involves gathering detailed information about your child from a range of people who know him or her. These people include you, the teachers, an educational psychologist and an officer of the Health Authority. Others who have relevant information and advice may also contribute, such as your child's doctor, specialist teachers, speech therapist, paediatrician, psychiatrist, home tutor, education welfare officer or social worker.

Statutory Assessment is generally requested by you or the school when you feel that your child's needs can only be met with additional, external support and resources which go beyond what the school can provide. The LEA is responsible for co-ordinating this process but parents play a key part and should be provided with information and advice from the LEA's *Named Officer* dealing with the case. The LEA should, in consultation with you, identify a *Named Person* who can help and advise you and accompany you to meetings. The Named Person might be a friend or relative, another parent with experience of the process, or someone from a voluntary association.

Once all information has been received, the LEA must decide whether to produce a *Statement of Special Educational Needs*. If it decides that a Statement is not necessary, it must provide you with reasons and produce a *Note in Lieu* which should include all the reports on your child.

The Statement describes in detail the nature of your child's difficulties and the help that must be provided. It also sets out educational targets that your child can be expected to achieve with the help provided, and arrangements for regular reviewing of progress.

The Statement will name a school for your child (or describe how education will be provided otherwise than at school).

The named school could be a mainstream school or a special school which caters for particular needs. As parents you have the right to express a preference for the school to be named in your child's Statement. The LEA must agree to your preference as long as

- the school is suitable for your child's age, ability and needs
- your child's attendance would not unduly affect the education of others at the school
- it is an efficient use of the LEA's resources.

Parents can choose to send their child to a school which is not maintained by the LEA. However, if there is a suitable LEA school there is no legal duty on the LEA to place your child there or to pay any fees.

There should be plenty of opportunity for you to discuss your preference. The LEA takes the final decision as to which school to name in the Statement, but if you disagree with this (or with other elements in the Statement, or with a decision not to produce a Statement) you have the right to appeal to the Special Educational Needs Tribunal (see Appendix 4).

By law your child's Statement must be reviewed at least once a year to ensure that it still accurately describes your child's problems, abilities and needs and to look at progress towards expected targets.

Pupils with Statements may stay on at school until they are 19. Alternatively they may transfer to a College of Further Education. The review of the pupil's Statement at 14+ will have a special focus on planning for the future and should include people who can give advice on training, education and career options.

# Transferring to secondary school or moving schools

If your child has already been identified as having special educational needs and is about to transfer to secondary school or a new school, information about her needs should be passed on to the new school before she starts. Schools have different systems for doing this; it is worth asking about the process and about how you as parent can provide further information to the new school.

If your child has a Statement then you should talk to the Named Officer of the LEA about an appropriate secondary school at least by the Spring term of Year 6 in primary school. The Statement will be amended to name the next school and reflect any changes in the help that should be provided.

If you are moving out of the area and your child will need to change schools, you should keep the Named Officer informed so that appropriate arrangements can be made. If the move will take you into a new LEA then you and the Named Officer will need to make contact with the relevant officer in that LEA. The receiving LEA will take on the responsibility for maintaining your child's Statement. They should let you know within six weeks of receiving the Statement when they intend to review it, or whether they will reassess your child's needs.

# Simple ways that parents can help

Some parents get very involved in supporting and extending work that their child is doing at school. Not all parents can manage this level of involvement, but some simple things will make a tremendous difference to your child:

- spending time with your child: talking, listening and showing that you enjoy her company
- noticing and praising her achievements
- recognising that she may sometimes feel miserable, and respecting her feelings
- sharing your knowledge and observations with school staff.

## The experiences of parents

A recent survey in one LEA showed that parents of children with special educational needs found it particularly difficult and frustrating when there was poor communication between themselves and the school, LEA or other agencies. This included feeling unheard and patronised and lacking information. Other things they found difficult were lack of resources and delays in the process of identifying and meeting their child's needs.

What these parents found especially helpful were self-help strategies for supporting and valuing their children; good communications and individual support from the LEA and school; clear information (including learning about the legal aspects of special educational needs provision and the Code of Practice); opportunities to meet other parents to share views and the problems they faced; and to receive a diagnosis of their child's problems, including having a 'label' to put to the problem.

Parents' accounts suggest that it is easy to feel isolated when your child has a special educational need. Establishing contacts within the school, with other parents and with voluntary organisations can be very helpful in reducing this sense of isolation as well as supportive in terms of practical ways of helping you and your child.

Your local LEA, Social Services Department or Citizens Advice Bureau will have information about national and local groups who support parents and children with special educational needs. The organisation Contact a Family links families to each other and to local support and their address is given at the end of the chapter.

# *Enhancing learning and increasing self-esteem*

In this chapter we have already looked at a range of strategies and techniques for helping your child with homework, with revising for exams, with making up for being a boy or a girl, with making progress as an able child or as a child with special needs. To conclude, here are some other suggestions for you to think about. They are drawn from parenting programmes running in this country and abroad. They will not all appeal to you, nor will you agree with them all and in some cases it may not be possible for you to carry them out, but we hope that they will make you reflect upon your role as parents who genuinely want to help their children.

## Communication

- Practise Active Listening, i.e. really listening carefully and responding to whatever your children want to tell you. Do not be dismissive of anything they say: paraphrase what they have told you, probe gently for more information, check out that you have understood, get them to talk about how they *feel* about what has happened.
- Try using 'I' statements rather than 'you' statements. The way we talk to others can either build up their confidence or weaken it and how we talk to children affects the way they feel about themselves. 'You' messages can be belittling and blaming: 'You make me so cross' or 'Don't talk back to me like that' put the responsibility for your feelings on the other person. 'I' statements are more effective: 'I feel angry when you ...', 'I want us to be able to talk sensibly and calmly about this ...', 'I get nervous when you ride your bicycle without your helmet so I want you to wear it all the time, even if you're just going down to the shops.'
- When your children talk to you, give them your full attention, make sure your body language tells them you are listening (look at them, nod, smile), do not interrupt, do not jump in with advice, respect what your children say even if you do not agree.

## Lifelong learning: being a good role model

In the minds of children, a barrier can be created between them and parents because they think that parents think they know all the answers. Consider becoming a learner yourself. Go to a night class, learn a new skill, take part in an activity at which you have to work hard to make progress. Share your own learning difficulties and triumphs with your children, even if they laugh at your puny efforts. The way you approach learning and the fact that you are still doing it at your advanced age will be an encouragement to them. You will be a good role model of a lifelong learner, which is what they are going to have to be.

## Reading

The basis for success in so much of our learning is the skill of reading. We need to go on improving our reading skills and learning new words all our lives. Make books a daily part of your life and if you cannot afford to buy them, use the public library. Let your children see you reading in odd moments; tell them what you are reading and how much you are enjoying it. Encourage them to read newspapers with a healthy critical attitude. Discuss what is in the press; remind them that what they see printed is not necessarily absolutely true, it is written by human beings who are fallible, or who have their own prejudices.

## Spending time together

Children have always learned a great deal from playing games within the family setting. Many of today's parents of teenage children will have played word games and acting games in their own childhood. As well as being fun, such games were influential in developing memory, vocabulary and self-confidence. Although families still play games when children are young, they often fade out as children get older. Why not consider a return to these activities, especially as there is now such a range of family games available that there must be something to suit your tastes! Alongside all the commercial games, consider looking at a workbook for parents and children produced by a consultant called Geoff Hannan, details of which can be found at the end of this chapter.

## Controlling television

Television has profoundly changed our lives, and technological advances such as cable, satellite and digital television make it likely to play an even greater part in everyday living. Keep it under control; use it for what it does best – bringing world events into our sitting-rooms, presenting issues in a striking and persuasive way, offering a wide range of entertainment. Do not allow it to dominate. Set the example to your children by not leaving the television on unless you are actually giving the programme your full attention. Plan to watch a programme and then turn the set off. If you watch a programme with your children, talk about it afterwards. If it is not a good programme, turn it off. As with newspapers, television programmes are made by fallible if talented human beings with prejudices of their own. Even something as apparently objective as the selection of news items is a reflection of what somebody considers to be important in the world.

If your children have access to television in their own rooms, talk with them about how they can control their viewing. Excessive watching of television appears to numb the brain, quite apart from effects of the content and value of the programmes themselves. An average young person of 15 will have spent more time watching television than being in school and will probably have witnessed 15,000 killings.

## Building up self-esteem

Every parent has the natural desire for their children to be as successful and happy as possible but the pursuit of success must be tempered in such a way that it never appears that their love and approval of their children depend on their children's success.

Every child in a family is unique and of equal value: never compare siblings.

Enjoy your children's achievements, however large or small, and remember that they are *their* achievements not yours, even though you may have enabled them to happen. Help your child to feel good and appreciated by praising the good things he or she does rather than by dwelling on the disappointments or failures.

# Further reading

**Confident children, a parents' guide to helping children feel good about themselves,** Gael Lindenfield, Thorsons, ISBN 0 7225 2824 8.

**Help your child with a foreign language,** Opal Dunn, Hodder and Stoughton, ISBN 0 340 60766 1. In the 'Positive Parenting' series.

**Help your child with homework and exams,** Jennie Lindon, Hodder and Stoughton. In the 'Positive Parenting' series, ISBN 0 340 65866 5.

**Help your child with maths,** Sue Atkinson, Hodder and Stoughton, ISBN 0 340 60767 X. In the 'Positive Parenting' series, this is mainly for parents of primary age children but it has a final chapter on Maths in Key Stage 3.

**Highly able girls and boys,** Joan Freeman, published by the Department for Education and Employment with NACE. Tel: 0171 510 0150.

**Information problem-solving: the Big Six skills approach to library and information skills instruction,** Michael B Eisenberg and Robert E Berkowitz, Norwood NJ, Ablec Publishing, 1990, ISBN 0 89391 7575.

**The secrets of success, a parent and child workbook,** Geoff Hannan, Training and Consultancy International, Bank Cottage, Bourton Road, Much Wenlock, Shropshire TF13 6AJ. Tel: 01952 727332.

## Special needs

**Meeting special educational needs: a summary of Part 3 of the 1993 Education Act,** Centre for Studies on Inclusive Education, 1994, 1 Redland House, Elm Lane, Redland, Bristol BS6 6UE. Tel: 0117 923 6450.

**Special Educational Needs: a guide for parents,** Department for Education and Employment.

**Statements: a handbook for parents in England and Wales,** Network 81, 1995, 1–7 Woodfield Terrace, Stansted, Essex CM24 8AJ. Tel: 01279 647415.

**Your child with special needs,** Susan Kerr, Hodder and Stoughton, ISBN 0 340 64764 7. In the 'Positive Parenting' series.

# Useful organisations

**Contact a Family** A charity linking families of children with special needs to each other and to local support. Tel: 0171 383 3555.

**Dyslexia Institute,** 133 Gresham Road, Staines, Middlesex TW18 2AJ. Tel: 01784 463851.

**Equal Opportunities Commission,** Overseas House, Quay Street, Manchester M3 3HN. Tel: 0161 833 9244.

**National Association for Gifted Children,** Elder House, Elder Gate, Milton Keynes MK9 1LR. Tel: 01908 673677. Provides services to parents and their gifted children.

**National Association for Able Children in Education,** The NACE Office, Room L6, Westminster College, Oxford OX2 9AT. Tel: 01865 245657. Provides services predominantly to schools, to help them improve their curriculum for able children.

**The National Bureau for Students with Disabilities (SKILL),** 336 Brixton Road, London SW9 7AA. Tel: 0171 274 0565.

# CHAPTER FIVE

# Getting the most out of secondary school

In the preceding chapters we have been looking at how young people are taught in secondary schools and how they learn at school and at home. We have focused on how parents can support the learning process including homework and revision. Success at secondary school depends on other factors as well – what might loosely be called 'having a positive attitude.

In this chapter we will look at how the following factors can have an influence on pupils' overall performance:

- diet and health
- bullying
- involvement in school life.

## *Diet and health*

The precise links between what we eat, how we feel and our daily performance are difficult for lay people to establish. The medical complexity is beyond the scope of a book like this but there is evidence, based on research by dietitians and on the every-day observation of teachers, that diet affects the way children behave.

Common sense tells us that children who are in good health and have a well-balanced diet are more likely to achieve the best they are capable of. Only in unusual cases which require specialist medical advice do adolescents need to follow a special diet. Indeed, obsession with diet can become a danger in itself and there have been well-publicised cases of girls who try to eat as little as possible and suffer from anorexia nervosa, or others who binge on food and them make themselves sick, a condition known as bulimia. These conditions are not confined to girls but boy sufferers are still only a small percentage. If you think that your child is suffering from either of these conditions, get advice from your GP.

It is important for children, as for adults, to have a substantial breakfast. Those who come to school hungry do not learn as well as those who have had a good breakfast, and research has confirmed that children who skip breakfast entirely are likely to become apathetic and irritable as their metabolic rate drops. What exactly constitutes a nutritious breakfast will depend upon family patterns and culture but in general, a breakfast with cereals, bread, fruit, milk, yoghurt and possibly eggs, cold meat or fish is ideal. It is not, however, a good idea to eat a traditional English fried breakfast every day. The increased metabolic rate that results from eating breakfast will actually reduce weight, an argument which might be used with teenagers who think it is fattening.

Most secondary schools organise their day with two breaks and it is sensible for eating to be split between the two. If your child devours all his lunch at morning break he will feel very hungry by mid-afternoon, just as if he does not eat until lunch he may find his attention wandering in late morning.

What your children eat during the school day is a critical issue for most parents. In most schools, there is no formal set meal and pupils queue up to serve themselves in a cafeteria. In addition, many schools run tuck shops with a wide range of food including chocolate, crisps and fizzy drinks. Vending machines have been installed in some secondary schools. On-site vending to pupils is sometimes done to prevent or discourage them from going off-site to the local shop where control by staff is difficult or impossible. Schools can also make a profit out of running a tuck shop and even though the money raised is tiny compared with the overall cost of running a school, every little helps. The issue is: what should a school sell at its tuck shop? Popular wisdom is that chocolate, crisps and fizzy drinks, especially if consumed as the principal elements of a daily diet, can make young people hyperactive, noisy and generally uncooperative. Yet if tuck shops ban such items and only sell healthy items, such as fruit, muesli bars and bread rolls, pupils stop on the way to school to stock up with unhealthy food, much of which contains sugar which is very bad for teeth.

What can you do? The most important influence comes from the pattern of eating at home. If this has been balanced, there is a greater likelihood that children will have learned good eating habits. The scope for parental intervention in what children eat during the day is limited. You can provide a packed lunch, or see that your child prepares his own lunch from suitable ingredients. You can limit the amount of money you give your child to buy what might be seen as extras. In some schools, it is possible for parents to buy meal tickets which can only be traded in for a balanced meal.

The topic of eating habits is one which parents need to broach with their children without letting it develop into a battleground. They will certainly be receiving good advice from school in lessons, which will probably be very similar to the guidelines published by the British Heart Foundation (see p104).

As far as drinks are concerned, water is highly recommended, as is skimmed or semi-skimmed milk. Decaffeinated coffee is preferable to standard coffee and full-fat drinking chocolate should be used sparingly. Fizzy drinks with sugar have been shown to have a harmful effect on behaviour as well as on teeth.

| Food type | Eat more of these | Eat less of these (keep for an occasional treat) |
| --- | --- | --- |
| **Cereals and bread** should form the main part of your diet | Wholemeal/wholegrain products, flour and bread, rice, pasta, breakfast cereals | Fancy bread, pastries (e.g. croissants), cream crackers |
| **Meat and fish** Lean meats should be chosen. Trim off any fat | Chicken, turkey, lean ham, sardines, tuna, white fish | Sausages, pate, meat pies, any fish fried in batter |
| **Dairy food and eggs** Low-fat alternatives are preferable to full-fat products | Skimmed and semi-skimmed milk, cottage cheese, low-fat yoghurt | Full cream milk, condensed milk, cream, most blue cheeses, hard cheeses e.g. Cheddar |
| **Fats and oils** Use these as little as possible | Polyunsaturated margarines and oils (e.g. corn oil, sunflower oil), olive oil, low fat spreads | Butter, dripping, lard, margarines not labelled as high in polyunsaturates |
| **Fruit and vegetables** A good source of dietary fibre and contain minerals and vitamins (five portions per day recommended) | Fresh is best! Most kinds of dried, canned and frozen fruits are fine too | Crisps, chips cooked in oil other than olive oil, avocados, fruits in syrup with added sugar |
| **Cakes, biscuits and desserts** should be avoided as much as possible | Low fat recipe cakes, jelly, sorbets, skimmed milk puddings | Ready-made cakes and biscuits, cream cakes, dairy ice-cream, full-fat milk puddings |

If these guidelines are followed, it is unlikely that supplementary vitamins or minerals will be needed but if in doubt, seek further specialised guidance.

# *Physical activity*

We all know that physical exercise is good for us yet many of us are increasingly reluctant to do it. Exercise increases the supply of oxygen and nutrients circulated by the lungs and heart to the brain. After physical activity which makes them perspire or breathe deeply, children are more alert and ready to learn.

All secondary schools must have a Physical Education programme which will go some way towards meeting your child's physical needs. The balance within a PE programme between competitive team sports and personal physical development varies somewhat from school to school. Some politicians would have us believe that team sports are the way to redeem the nation's youth but the reality is that some young people do not like competing because they do not like losing all the time or feeling that they are being made to look silly or inadequate. Some regularly try to find excuses for not taking part: 'forgetting their kit' or 'beginning a cold' are among the most frequent. It really does not help your child to connive at this avoidance of Physical Education.

Once again the example you set is paramount. If you enjoy activities like swimming, cycling, walking, dancing, jogging, skating or skiing, your children will be more likely to take part in such activities too. At a more mundane level, if you always take your children everywhere by car, they will grow up to be dependent upon you and the car. Perhaps you – and certainly your own parents – walked several miles to school every day. Very few children do so today, as the traffic jams outside every school in the country morning and evening testify. Once again, the British Heart Foundation advice is worth noting:

- walk to the shops instead of taking the car
- try taking the stairs instead of the lift
- try to walk somewhere vigorously for at least twenty minutes three times a week.

Walking to school with an adult is a good way for young children to learn road sense. Walking to secondary school with a group of friends gives valuable physical exercise and is a bonding experience.

## Smoking

Although the dangers of smoking are so well known and even though health education in schools is more fully developed than ever before, the incidence of smoking in young people is on the increase again. Fewer adults smoke now than twenty years ago but teenagers are proving impervious to anti-smoking messages. Girls are smoking in larger numbers than boys although it has to be added that a girl smoker generally smokes fewer cigarettes per week than a boy.

Smoking is in a sense linked to other aspects of substance abuse such as alcohol and drugs. These are dealt with in Chapter 8 but we are considering smoking in this chapter because it is a more common problem.

Understandably, medical and education professionals are worried about the trend towards more smoking by young women. Those who smoke when they are pregnant generally produce smaller babies and the link with children's poor health and slower development is well established.

The issue of smoking and young people is one that cannot simply be ignored. Even though the sale of tobacco to young people under 16 has been tightened through recent legislation, the advertising lobby for smoking is powerful and effective. What can you do as a parent?

### *Be aware of the facts*

Make sure that you are up to date with all the information about the effects of smoking: that it causes over 100,000 premature deaths a year in the UK alone and contributes to cancer and heart disease and aggravates many other physical ailments; that it adds enormously to the cost of the nation in terms of health care and time lost from work; that nicotine is a drug which is extremely difficult to give up (a concept that young teenagers find difficult to understand) and it is therefore far harder to stop than you realise.

The link between smoking and lower academic performance is well substantiated but it is not easy to disentangle cause and effect. If it is true that the academic performance of smokers is lower than non-smokers, is it because people of lower ability are attracted to smoking, or is it the act of smoking itself which depresses performance? Nicotine is both a stimulant and a depressant and can stop you thinking clearly. Our personal judgement about the link between smoking and academic performance tends to be confused if we happen to know individuals who are smokers and who are highly intelligent and academically successful.

## Understand why children start smoking

Up to about the age of 9, children have a strong moral view of the world based on what parents, teachers and other role models have told them. They sort things out easily according to what is good and bad. Smoking generally falls on the 'bad' list. By the time they reach ten to 12 years, many experiment with smoking. In the new social situation of secondary school, smoking can appear to be a useful device for finding a niche in the social order. People are particularly vulnerable to starting smoking at times of transition in their lives.

Cigarettes can become for young people a way of defining who they are, rather like music, clothes and posters. They can be used to manage the moods which are associated with puberty; it is believed that they calm nerves, ease stress and relieve boredom. The cleverest technique of cigarette advertising has been to link smoking with a romantic image, and with feeling tough or looking sophisticated.

For many young people, the pressure to do what others of their age are doing is irresistibly powerful. They do not want to be left behind on the adventurous journey into adulthood. Smoking is a way of separating themselves from parents, from the school system (which may be why those having least success in it are more likely to smoke) and from younger children. Smoking becomes a social passport and cigarettes a valuable currency in the business of building friendships.

The pressures outlined above are more powerful than anti-smoking propaganda which emphasises the physical dangers. Teenagers are rarely put off smoking by the thought of getting cancer because they cannot conceptualise the idea of getting old. They also think, mistakenly, that they are only smoking a few – 'just a social smoker' – and so it will be easy to give up. They are intellectually aware of the possibility of physical dependency but not emotionally convinced.

## *Be prepared to talk about it*

Elsewhere in this book we have emphasised the importance of trying to keep the lines of communication open between you and your children. If you take a genuine interest in what they do, if you listen to them, there will be a greater chance that you can talk over the problems too. Rather than delivering the heavy lecture, or getting very upset, or threatening punitive action, it seems to be better to talk it over, explaining calmly but clearly why you are concerned. It is because you love your children that you do not want to see them wilfully harming themselves. You want to know what it is that is making them want to smoke, and this may guide you in finding ways of filling whatever gaps in their lives or self-esteem may emerge. The same advice given in an earlier chapter applies here: remember that it is the smoking you dislike and disapprove of, not them as individuals.

## *If you are a smoker yourself*

Parents who are themselves smokers are often particularly diffident about broaching this subject and feel that they cannot dissuade their children from smoking without being accused of hypocrisy. Research in Canada has shown, however, that it is particularly important for smoking parents to try to influence their children against smoking. The children of smoking parents who actively discourage their children from smoking are twice as likely to start than the children of non-smoking parents, whereas the children of smoking parents who ignore the issue are seven times more likely to start.

The most effective way is to be completely honest: tell them how and why you started; without excusing the behaviour, tell them that there is much more proof today of the harm caused by smoking than there was when you started. Share with them your experience of the addictive power of nicotine and the difficulty of giving up. Be candid in asking your children not to make the same mistakes you have made and perhaps you might even try giving up yourself. It would certainly be helpful if you tried not to smoke in a car or in a room where there are babies, young children or anyone who cannot escape from inhaling your smoke.

## Physical illness

A small minority of children may have to have time off school because of an accident or an illness. Try to find ways in which your sick child can keep in touch with the work that he is missing, but do not force him to do schoolwork at home while he convalesces until he is clearly ready to do so. If you can, persuade friends to call on him regularly, bringing him information about the work that has been done but, more importantly, to tell him about school, including a bit of gossip, so that he will not feel so isolated on his return. Paediatric wards generally have a hospital-based teacher who will liaise with teachers and parents over appropriate work.

### *ME*

A few children suffer from an illness called myalgic encephalomyelitis (ME) which differs from other more obvious illnesses in not having physically identifiable symptoms, other than that the victim feels exhausted. There is a growing awareness in schools of this condition although it is difficult for teachers, doctors and parents to distinguish it from routine idleness or apathy. ME sufferers know that they are not being deliberately lazy but it is not always easy to convince others.

For parents of a child with ME, it is essential to have confidence that your child is going to get better and to convey this to your child. Schoolwork can still be done, but it must be paced. It may be possible to go to school for part of the day but the teachers need to know that the ME sufferer may have to rest during the day. As with the more obvious physical illnesses referred to above, it is important that the child absent from school for long periods does not lose social contact. Visits from friends are essential, provided they are brief and designed to cheer the victim up, rather than to depress him by making him more conscious of how much work he is missing.

A good and caring school will make special arrangements to send work home or to arrange for exams to be taken at home or to be staged over a period of years rather than all taken at once. Parents with a child suffering from ME, or from any long-term or debilitating illness such as glandular fever, must keep in close touch with the tutor, or Head of Year, so that the necessary flexible arrangements can be made for keeping some contact with academic work and with the educational journey. If your child is likely to be off school for a long period, the LEA may provide a home tutor who will agree a programme of tuition with you and the school.

Perhaps the most important part of the process of recovery, short or long though it may be, is for young people to know that the school has not forgotten them and that everybody has confidence that they will pull through and lead a full and rewarding life.

## Menstruation

The majority of girls start their periods during the secondary school years.

It is obviously important that girls have clear knowledge of what will happen to their bodies during puberty and when they begin to menstruate. Although your daughter may gain much information from her friends and from magazines, you cannot assume that her knowledge is complete or accurate. Surveys have shown that girls want their parents to provide them with this information so do not delay in discussing this subject with your daughter. There are many helpful pamphlets and books for young people (see the list at the end of the chapter). Your GP and school nurse will also be willing to advise you.

As well as factual information, your daughter may need advice and help with buying sanitary pads when she first starts her periods. Not all schools are equally sensitive to the needs of menstruating girls. You may need to check that she has somewhere to keep pads and whether they can be easily obtained in school. You could raise this discreetly with the school if you feel that arrangements could be improved.

Lastly, it is important for the family to realise that, although menstruation is not an illness, some girls suffer from pre-menstrual tension and can feel quite ill during their periods, with cramps, headaches and faintness. They can be moody and sensitive at these times and will need understanding and tact.

# *Bullying*

A young person who is unhappy at school because they are frightened cannot possibly make the most of the opportunities available. Bullying is a block to learning and a source of great unhappiness and must be taken seriously.

Although bullying receives much more media attention than it used to and has become an issue about which people will talk more openly, it is by no means certain that it is any more prevalent today than it was a generation ago. About 15 per cent of children in school are involved in bullying at some time in their school lives (9 per cent as victims, 6 per cent as bullies).

As well as the obvious physical threats, bullying can take other forms: name-calling, rumour-mongering, gestures, isolation and graffiti are all unpleasant ways for one person to seek to control and dominate others. Girls have been shown to use the more covert approach of verbal bullying; boys tend to be more physical.

Racist name-calling is insidious because it not only insults the individual victims but also their family, community and culture. Racist behaviour in schools can also take the form of wearing offensive badges or insignia, bringing in provocative magazines or leaflets, ridicule of people's dress, food or music, and refusing to sit next to or work with a child because of his ethnic group.

Racial and sexual harassment are particularly distressing forms of bullying and schools should have policies in place which require them to monitor such activities closely and to act firmly in dealing with them. Parents should have no hesitation in reporting incidents of this kind. Equally, do not let racist or sexist remarks or jokes from your own child go unchecked as this suggests that the ideas they contain are acceptable.

The main reassurance for parents is to know that most schools take bullying seriously. What used to be accepted as part of the rough-and-tumble of everyday life in school is now seen for what it is – anti-social behaviour which is bad for the victim and for the bully. Many schools have developed an anti-bullying policy, often with the involvement of pupils themselves. It is now much more acceptable to 'tell' on another pupil who is making life miserable for others.

How might you know if your child is being bullied? Your child may not want to go to school, or be looking for health excuses for having time off. Some are physically ill with headaches, stomach ache and cramps. They may become listless and withdrawn, not wanting to talk about school. Other indicators are:

- frequently lost equipment, clothing or personal belongings
- scrawling on books, exercise books, pencil cases
- nightmares and anxiety late at night and in the morning
- anonymous telephone calls
- loss of weight or excessive comfort eating.

## How can parents help?

Helping your child to talk about what is going on is the first step to recovery. It may not be easy: possibly he feels a failure for having become a victim and he may also feel slightly guilty because his own behaviour towards others may not always have been ideal.

The tough-guy approach ('Stand up for yourself and hit them back') and the dismissive approach ('Don't be a wimp, it's all part of life, you'll get over it') are not recommended. Get your child to tell you when the bullying takes place, how it happens and who is involved. Reassure him that you want to help him find a way through this difficulty and that it is something from which he can emerge. Reassure him that he has your love and trust, but that you want to strengthen him so that he can find ways, in the first instance, of working through his problems by his own resources.

There are a number of strategies which can be suggested to a bullied child:

- do not attempt to buy yourself out of trouble by supplying the bully with sweets, cigarettes or by handing over money
- make sure that you are always with friends if you can foresee a situation where your tormentor may be expecting you
- teach yourself to walk away confidently (head up, shoulders back) from a difficult situation, keeping your bully in sight
- try positive and assertive talking ('I don't like it when you talk like that', 'I don't want to get into an argument with you', 'I have to get home quickly so I would like to get past, please')
- at break or lunchtimes (which is when most bullying takes place), try to stay within eyesight of the member of staff on

duty, or go to the library, work-room or to a club. Hanging around could be asking for trouble.

If the bullying is persistent and serious, do not hesitate to involve the staff in school. Make an appointment to go in to see the relevant teacher (possibly a form tutor, or a Head of Year) but do not rush in straight after an incident and in an emotional state. Make sure you have the precise details of the incident as it has been reported to you, be specific and do not expect an instant miracle. You may find out that your own child is not always above reproach in his behaviour towards others. The school should be able to tell you how they will deal with the problem because it will certainly not be the first time they have met this kind of situation.

## What can schools do?

If your child has been bullied, you may expect the school to take punitive action and many schools do take some measures to signal their disapproval of such conduct. Remember that the outcome which all should be seeking is a change in the behaviour of the bully as well as the safety of the bullied.

If it is your child who has been doing the bullying, it may be that they are copying older brothers or sisters, or other members of the family or adults whom they admire. They may be acting out some personal unhappiness in this aggressive way or they may be compensating for the low opinion they have of themselves. To stop your child from bullying, you must discourage those around him from using force or violent language to get what they want. You must keep checking with him that he is not resorting to bullying at school and give him lots of praise and encouragement when he is kind or co-operative towards others. Keep on building up his sense of self-worth.

At the end of any meeting with teachers in school, make sure that you understand what they are going to do and what they want you to do and in what time span. If there is no progress within the agreed time limit, it is perfectly in order for you to go to somebody higher up the system, for example a Deputy Head. If you feel that the school is not taking the matter seriously, you could refer the matter to a Governor or to the LEA (see Chapter 6). Whatever school your children attend, whether state or fee-paying, you have the right to see them treated with respect and able to learn in safety.

Many schools are now adopting a technique of getting pupils in conflict with each other to talk through their difficulties face to face, sometimes with both sets of parents present. Some schools are also encouraging awareness and self-help through peer group counselling. This can help both bullies and victims but needs careful teacher preparation and support.

In extreme cases of bullying where you have not been able to negotiate a satisfactory outcome, you may need to consider changing school, but keep this as a last resort. If you do decide to make contact with an alternative school, tell them honestly what the problem has been and they may be able to place your child so that somebody keeps a special eye on him.

Problems of bullying which occur outside school are sometimes dealt with by the school if the problem has arisen in school or is affecting relationships within school. You should not however expect the school to resolve bullying incidents which are unrelated to school. These should be dealt with, according to the seriousness of the incident, by an approach to the bully's parents, either directly if this can be done amicably and without danger, or through a third party mediator, or by reference to the police or by a solicitor's letter. The Citizens Advice Bureau will be able to give guidance.

Above all, encourage all your children to have positive thoughts about their own abilities, to feel self-confident and to make an effort to have friends of their own. To be part of a circle of genuine friends, including boys and girls and people of different ethnic backgrounds, is a good defence against victimisation.

# Involvement in school life

## Extra-curricular activities

Most secondary schools now offer a range of clubs and activities and you should certainly do everything you can to encourage your child to take part. The skills and talents which can be developed through participation in music, drama, sport, debating, the Duke of Edinburgh Award Scheme and community service will be very useful in adult life, as well as being enjoyable for their own sake.

Extra-curricular activities help to reinforce young people's positive feelings about life in school. It is not just about work, which they may or may not enjoy, but also about having other enjoyable things to do. Most clubs are run by teachers who are giving up their free time. Young people who meet teachers in this more informal context develop more positive attitudes to the staff and, if they remember to thank the member of staff for taking the club, can reinforce the warm feelings of the teacher towards the pupils. If the school does not offer a club for an activity on which your daughter and her friends are keen, why not suggest that they approach a teacher to help them set up a club for themselves? Organising such an activity is excellent practice for later life.

Some parents worry about the amount of time taken up by extra-curricular activities and fear that it might be interfering with schoolwork. As with adults, it is a question of balance and time-management. Learning to organise your life so that you can fit in a sports team, an orchestra rehearsal and still do your homework to a high standard is a challenge. Remarkably, many young people do it very well indeed and in so doing are learning the important skill of how to manage their time.

## Participation in the structure of the school

Experience shows that those pupils who are prepared to participate in school life get the most out of school. Besides hoping that pupils will join in extra-curricular activities, many schools now encourage pupils to express their opinions about school by being on a school council.

This involves them in standing for election, possibly by their tutor group or their Year group, making a speech, presenting their views and answering questions. Once elected, they will be expected to attend council meetings regularly, representing the views of other pupils as well as putting forward their own opinions. They will be able to meet teachers in a different context and will have the valuable experience of arguing in a civilised and controlled environment. They will be expected to feed back the outcome of the meetings they have attended to their fellow pupils.

This is an excellent opportunity for practising involvement in the democratic process and for developing the skills of public speaking and face-to-face negotiation. Young people who learn to look critically but constructively at the way their school is organised are on the way to becoming the leaders of the future. They are likely to make much more progress than those who simply accept (or reject) school as it is.

A good school will probably offer a range of participative opportunities:

- school council
- social events
- charity and fund-raising events
- community service outside school
- service within school (such as older pupils helping younger pupils by listening to them read, or by organising clubs and sporting activities).

If your daughter attends a school which is not yet developing along these lines, discuss with her how she and her friends might go about suggesting that such opportunities might be created. In so doing, she will be experiencing the important process of bringing about change in society or at least will be learning why change is not always as easily achieved as one might hope.

Secondary school offers young people the chance to grow up in many aspects of their life. Recent government policies have tended to emphasise academic success as the main or only criterion of a 'good education'. In this chapter we have tried to offer a counterbalance by suggesting that a good education in a secondary school involves the development of talents outside the classroom and of the personal skills of self-discipline, time management, good relations with others and commitment to the school as a community.

# Further reading

## Puberty and menstruation

**Boys looking ahead/Girls looking ahead,** two leaflets aimed at 9 to 11-year-olds to help them understand the changes that take place during puberty. Available from the Brook Advisory Centres. Tel: 0171 833 8488.

**Helping girls cope with menstruation in school,** Shirley Prendergast (1994). The Family Planning Association.

**Periods: what you need to know,** the Family Planning Association, available from Healthwise (see below).

**Sexuality and young people with learning difficulties,** K. Aram, (1995), from the Special Needs Sexuality Project. Tel: 0181 690 7438.

**The adolescent years: a guide for parents,** P. Petrie, Michael Joseph (1990). A comprehensive guide to all aspects of adolescence.

## Bullying

**Bullying – advice for parents,** ACE, in the 'My child in school' series. See Appendix 12 for ACE's address.

**Bullying: a positive response, advice for parents, Governors and staff in schools,** Delwyn Tattum and Graham Herbert, Cardiff Institute of Higher Education, Cyncoed Road, Cardiff CF2 6XD.

**Stop the bullying, a guide for parents,** Carrie Herbert, 49 New Square, Cambridge CB1 1EZ. Tel: 01223 366052.

## General

**Children's voices in school matters,** Laura Ashworth, ACE, ISBN 1 870672 25 9.

# Useful organisations

**ABC (Anti-Bullying Campaign),** Angela Glaser, 18 Elmgate Gardens, Edgware, Middlesex HA8 9RT.

**Action on Smoking and Health (ASH),** 12–15 Dartmouth Street, London SW1H. Tel: 0171 314 1360.

**Campaign for Anti-racist Education (CARE),** PO Box 68, London SW8 1SX.

**Childline,** Freepost 1111, London N1 0BR. Tel: Free 0800 1111.

**Commission for Racial Equality (CRE),** Elliott House, 10–12 Allington Street, London SW1E 5EH. Tel: 0171 828 7022.

**Eating Disorders Association,** General Helpline: 01603 621414; Youth Helpline: 01603 765050.

**Healthwise,** 2–12 Pentonville Road, London, N1 9FP. Tel: 0171 837 5432. This is the book service of the Family Planning Association.

**Kidscape** – campaigns for children's personal safety and the prevention of bullying, 152 Buckingham Palace Road, London SW1 9TR.

**ME Association,** Stanhope House, High Street, Stanford le Hope, Essex SS17 0HA.

**Sex Education Forum,** National Children's Bureau, 8 Wakley Street, London, EC1V 7QE. Tel: 0171 843 6052.

CHAPTER SIX

# Parents and schools in partnership

So far we have been looking closely at how you can support your child as an individual going through secondary school, learning well and making the most of the opportunities available. In this chapter, we look at how parents can relate to the school as a whole and how they can develop a fruitful partnership between home and school, including how to go about resolving difficulties.

We discuss:

- information and communication
- complaining constructively
- parental involvement in the school community
- how schools are accountable to parents
- what parents need to know about the school's finances.

# Information and communication

## Receiving information from school

The quantity and quality of information available for parents from schools has improved in the last few years. Schools are required to produce a detailed prospectus giving information about procedures, policies and achievements. Additionally, at each stage of your child's career in secondary school, you should receive separate brochures about options choices, careers and examination procedures. Many schools also issue regular newsletters giving reports on past events, details of forthcoming activities, perspectives on national educational issues and messages for parents.

Much of this information is brought home by your child. It is a good idea to establish from the beginning of his time in secondary school the importance of remembering to hand over information to you on the day it is distributed. This is an essential feature of home-school communication and nothing is more frustrating than to come across a crumpled letter at the bottom of a bag days after an event has taken place.

Many schools operate a day book or diary arrangement whereby pupils note their homework and other messages on a daily basis. Remember to sign this regularly so that the form tutor knows that you are receiving the information and are acting upon it.

Your child's school will send home a written report on her at least once a year, sometimes with interim progress checks between full reports. The format of reports has been developing over recent years and the days of the single sheet with one-line comments are disappearing. You will find that the reports give you a very full statement of your children's progress, behaviour, attitude and potential. In many schools the pupils write a self-assessment, either on each subject or on their overall performance in school. It is worth devoting your best attention to reports because the teachers will have invested a great deal of time in writing them. It is perfectly in order for you to follow up what a teacher has said by asking for clarification or further detail. Teachers will welcome the fact that you have read the report thoroughly and thought about it.

## Parents' evenings

Schools will offer parents one or more occasions in the year when they can have a personal interview with the subject teachers and form tutor. Not all teachers or parents find these occasions easy or comfortable but it is an essential part of the process of communication between home and school. You will probably be given an appointment and the time available will be specified. In order to get the most out of the relatively short time allowed, think about the process in advance.

- Discuss the subjects with your child and find out how he feels about his progress.
- Write down any specific questions you want to ask the teachers.
- During your meeting with each teacher, make notes if you wish to remember key points. It is surprising how it all becomes a blur after a long evening of waiting to see teachers interspersed with intensive talking.
- If your child is finding the subject difficult, it is best to be honest about your worries so that the teacher can give specific guidance on how things might improve.
- If a serious problem emerges during the interview, arrange to meet the teacher on a different occasion to explore the matter further. It is difficult to concentrate on a crisis when you know there is a queue of other parents waiting behind you to see the same teacher.

Although many parents may be confident and effective within their own business or workplace, there may still be a tendency to feel awed or intimidated by 'experts' within other systems. A good teacher will of course put you at your ease but you may still feel reluctant to express your opinion for fear that you may be blamed or made to feel inferior. Try to adopt a collaborative approach, remembering that the whole purpose of the exercise is to share information about your child's learning and to make it more effective.

After the parents' evening, discuss what you have been told frankly with your child, follow up any specific steps which have been suggested and keep your notes so that you can review them before you go to the next parents' evening. The time invested by you and teachers in this consultation is precious and it is essential that you do your best never to miss a parents' evening. If you are unable to attend, most schools will arrange for you to meet any teachers you particularly need to see on another occasion. Some schools encourage parents of older pupils to bring them along to join in the conversation and so make them active participants in their own learning – if you are offered this opportunity it is well worth taking up.

## Open evenings

Many schools mount exhibitions of pupils' work or put on evenings where a department demonstrates the work it is doing. These are invaluable occasions for you to find out about the work being done in the school and will enable you to support your child's learning more effectively simply by being better informed about it.

Even though such open evenings are not an occasion for you to enquire about the progress being made by your own individual child, they are excellent opportunities to meet the teachers. It encourages pupils taking part in an open evening to see their own and other parents there. It is also supportive to the teachers who will have put a lot of effort into getting the evening ready. Teachers are after all human beings who respond better when they know that their efforts are appreciated.

## Home–school partnership agreements

There is a growing trend to make the relationship between home and school more explicit and detailed. Some advocate the use of the word 'contract' although it has to be recognised that the enforceability of contracts in the legal sense would be difficult and indeed counter-productive in a school setting.

Nevertheless it can be valuable to have a clear statement of what everybody can reasonably expect of each other. The aim of the exercise would be to:

- reinforce the concept that a successful school stems from a meaningful partnership between Governors, teachers, parents and pupils
- ensure that all the partners are clear about their roles and responsibilities
- create an environment in which pupils behave appropriately
- enable young people to take a measure of responsibility for their own learning and personal development.

For example, the school might have the following expectations of parents and pupils:

- support for the aims and ethos of the school
- punctuality and regular attendance
- preparedness and co-operation for learning
- behaviour which does not disrupt the learning of others
- respect for staff, for one another, for property and belongings
- good liaison with school regarding concerns about a pupil's progress, behaviour or relationships.

At the same time, pupils and parents might have the following expectations of the school:

- a safe and secure environment where learning can prosper
- an ethos in which pupils are valued as individuals and where there is no discrimination on the grounds of race, colour, gender or disability
- work which meets the needs of the individual
- work which is conscientiously marked
- regular and clear information on school structures and on individual progress
- sympathetic and fair consideration of parental or pupil concerns
- formally structured arrangements for parents to meet teachers.

In practice, most schools adopt the above policies but not all are explicit about them. The process of arriving at a home–school partnership agreement should involve all the interested parties and should in itself make a useful contribution to a better understanding between home and school.

## Child protection

Schools have a specific legal responsibility in the area of child protection. This means that school staff have to be aware of and vigilant for any signs of physical, emotional or sexual abuse, or neglect. The school is under an obligation to report any suspected abuse to Social Services.

Schools themselves do not carry out investigations or intervene in cases of abuse. However, they must co-operate with the police and Social Services who follow up any suspected abuse.

The fact that the school must put the interests of children first in cases of suspected abuse means that, on occasion, where the suspicion turns out to have been unfounded, parents can be very upset and angry. This is an unfortunate situation but one which is bound to occur occasionally. The school's first responsibility is to protect a child about whom they have worries. Their priority is to act on their concerns rather than to save parents' feelings.

# Complaining constructively

Things will inevitably crop up from time to time that make you annoyed or upset with the school. Some issues you will let pass, but there may be a problem that is so continuous or serious that you feel you must take it up with the school.

You are perfectly entitled to raise concerns with your school. Indeed, a school which regards its parents as partners will welcome this if you do it in a constructive way, because it will want to sort out any problem you or your child have, and because this is one way of improving the quality of its service.

The key to a positive outcome is a positive approach. If you go blazing up to the school and insist on seeing the Head, and then regale her with your disgust and dismay at the shortcomings of her school, you are unlikely to elicit the best response. Most of us become defensive when attacked. Try to describe clearly what you are unhappy about without making accusations or seeming aggressive. If you are angry with the school, wait until you have calmed down before you decide what to do.

Before you take any action at all, think through:

- What exactly has happened/is happening that annoys or upsets you?
- What is your evidence for believing this? Check your facts.
- Which member of staff is responsible for dealing with your problem?
- What do you want to happen as a result of your complaint – and is this a constructive and reasonable expectation?

Most concerns can be sorted out quickly and effectively through informal discussion with your child's class teacher, form tutor, Head of Year or Head of House. The general principle, as we explained in Chapter 2, is to speak to the member of staff 'nearest' the problem.

Remember that the school will want to resolve problems as

much as you do, but things can't always change overnight. You may have to trust them to make changes or try new approaches and then give it time to work.

When you have a meeting with a member of staff it may help you both to make a note of any action that you have agreed, and in some cases, to arrange another meeting to review progress.

If you find it difficult to express yourself in these situations, or if you do not share the same first language as the teacher, it might help to bring along a friend, an Education Welfare Officer or a translator for support. Sometimes it is useful to have someone else there to mediate.

For particularly serious or sensitive issues parents can write to or arrange a meeting with the Headteacher, but in general, secondary school heads delegate the first stages of liaison with parents to a deputy head or senior member of staff. If you feel that your concern has not been properly addressed, you should then ask to see the Head about it. In the end, if you and the school cannot agree on something, you must decide how important it is, and whether it is for your own or your child's benefit that you are pursuing the issue. After a point it is unproductive for both parties to continue to rehearse a disagreement.

If you feel dissatisfied with the way the Head has responded to a problem you can complain to the Chair of Governors. You'll find the address in the Annual Report to Parents, or you can send your letter (marked 'confidential') c/o the Clerk to Governors via the school office. Some governing bodies have a Complaints Committee; others will arrange for one or more Governors to look into your complaint.

For LEA schools there is usually a local authority Education Officer with whom you can discuss difficult issues connected with school. The Education Officer may be able to help sort out your problem in liaison with the school.

Beyond the LEA, the Local Government Ombudsman (get the address from your local Citizens Advice Bureau) and the Secretary of State for Education and Employment (see Appendix 12 for the address) both have limited powers to intervene where a governing body (whether LEA or Grant Maintained) has not exercised its powers reasonably or is failing to carry out its duties. It is relatively rare that things reach this stage. Complaints to these bodies can result in a review of the situation by the school. However, complaint to an external body can cause a souring of relationships with the school. It is worth checking with yourself at each stage of your complaint, 'what do I want to get out of this and is this the best way of getting there?'.

If, in the end, you are not satisfied with the education your child's school is providing or with some other aspect of your child's school experience, you are entitled to transfer her to another school (as long as it has a place to offer). The other school will probably want to know why you are moving your child, but the offer of a place should not be affected by your reason (see Chapter 1 on Admissions). Headteachers will generally expect you to have told the Head of your child's present school before you request a transfer into their school. Transfer to a new school can be highly disruptive to a child's education, but in some cases it provides a fresh start or a better match with parents' expectations. It is not a decision to be taken hastily.

## Curriculum complaints

If your complaint is specifically about the curriculum or the provision of Religious Education or Worship (but not about individual teachers), there is a Curriculum Complaints Procedure set out by the Education Act 1988 which you should follow. This is explained in Appendix 8.

# Parental involvement in the school community

Schools need you to be involved both for your own child's sake and for that of the school as a community. The channel for this support is usually a Parent Teacher Association (PTA) or a Parents' Association or Friends of the School. Although there are PTAs in most primary schools, there appears to be less activity of this nature in the secondary sector. Perhaps it is because parents feel that their help is no longer needed in a larger school, or that they are going through a busier phase in their own working lives. Some teenagers have been known to discourage their parents from being seen to be publicly involved with secondary school because it is embarrassing!

Secondary schools which have succeeded in involving parents recognise what an important contribution they can make to the life of the school. In many cases, parents help with social and fund-raising activities. Although these can only make a relatively minor contribution to the finances of a school, they can add enormously to the morale of the place. Teachers are greatly heartened to receive extra items of equipment for their teaching which have been provided by the PTA.

The scope for practical assistance is enormous. Volunteers from the parents, if efficiently co-ordinated, can provide help with, say, repairing text-books, redecorating classrooms, mending curtains, serving refreshments at school events and many other practical projects around the site. Committed parents in a school in Australia decided that the Year 11 pupils needed a social centre so, with the support of the Principal and relevant planning permission, they raised funds to buy a transportable building which they delivered, erected, decorated, equipped and furnished in a weekend!

Despite the fact that many parents have valuable knowledge and skills to share, classroom help from parents is less common in the secondary sector than in the primary. Nevertheless some schools involve parents with the Learning Support Department, or get parents with appropriate qualifications to help with running sports teams, driving the minibus, accompanying school trips, supervising children back-stage in productions and providing occasional clerical help.

The skills, expertise and dedication of parents of secondary age pupils is a largely untapped source so if the school your child attends has not got an effective PTA, why not set about helping to make it work? The secret of success is to get a lot of people giving a small amount of time and energy, rather than to expect a very small group to do everything.

Perhaps the most important area of activity for a PTA is to be involved in educational matters. If there is as yet no forum in which parents can discuss with the school issues of general educational significance (as distinct from their own children as individuals), perhaps you might consider, with the help of like-minded parents, approaching the Headteacher to see if one could be set up. Schools which have attempted this have found it to be rewarding: it brings good ideas into school from the parents and gives the school a chance to consult the parents on any proposals it may have for change. Many of the topics covered in this book could be fruitfully discussed in an educational forum.

A secondary school in which parents are encouraged to be involved in all aspects of the school's life, in an organised and structured way, is greatly enriched. If we have stressed in this section the help you can give to the school by being active in the PTA, you may be further encouraged by the thought that, when you leave the comfort of your home to go out to a PTA event, you are giving your own child an important message, even though you may never put it into words. You are saying that your child's education matters to you so much that you want to do what you can to help the school. Children with a parent committed in this way will more often than not respond by having a similarly positive attitude, and their work and progress will be all the better for it.

# How schools are accountable to parents

The last 15 years have brought about much greater accountability in the education system. Schools are open to public scrutiny in a variety of ways and, quite apart from the voluntary input advocated above, parents are legally entitled to certain information and involvement.

## The governing body

All secondary schools have a governing body which has a great deal of responsibility for the overall policy and direction of the school, even though the day-to-day management and discipline of the school remain with the Headteacher and staff. There are at least four parent Governors (more in the case of Grant Maintained schools) and they are elected for a four-year term of office. Being a parent Governor is an excellent way of making a positive contribution to the development of the school; you might want to stand for election when the opportunity arises.

The Governors meet regularly at least once a term and have a number of committees to consider different aspects of the life of the school. Every year they have to give an account of their work to the parents. This is done by the *Annual Report*, which is sent home to every parent and has to include, amongst other things, information about:

- who the Governors are and how they can be contacted
- the school's academic results
- pupils' unauthorised absence rate
- the school's finances and details of any donations made
- information on school–community links (including the police)
- how the policy on special needs is being implemented
- the outcome of the Governors' consideration of whether or not to hold a ballot for GM (Grant Maintained) status

- arrangements for admitting pupils with disabilities.

Many schools will include very much more than the statutory requirements. The Annual Report will also include an invitation to the *Annual Parents' Meeting* at which parents can discuss the Report and the way in which the Governors, the Head and the LEA have carried out their functions in relation to the school. The Governors of GM schools have to hold a similar meeting but the procedures are slightly different.

The Annual Meeting is the formal opportunity for parents to raise any matters of concern (other than the criticism of individuals). If the number of parents present is at least 20 per cent of the number of pupils on roll, the meeting may pass a formal resolution on which the Governors have to act and report back the following year.

In practice, Annual Meetings have not been well attended and a number of schools have linked them in with some other school event.

The governing body can be approached at any time in the year, not just at the Annual Meeting. The Clerk to the Governors, whose name and address will be published in the Annual Report, will pass on letters to them. If you have a serious grievance with the school and have not been able to get it resolved by the staff, you may want to pass on your concern to the Governors or to the LEA.

## Publication of examination results

Part of the Government's drive to raise standards has been its belief that the publication of examination results will increase competition between schools and therefore bring about an improvement in results. There has been a general improvement in academic performance in recent years but it would be a rash person would who suggest a direct link between this improvement and the publication of results.

Every November, the papers carry the results of the preceding summer's examinations at GCSE, A Level and for advanced and intermediate vocational qualifications. For 16-year-olds, the tables show the proportion of the year group achieving five or more higher grades (A* to C), five or more A* to G grades and the proportion achieving at least one A* to G grade. For A Levels, the key statistic is the average number of points per candidate (A = 10, B = 8, C = 6, etc.). Another column shows the percentage of half day absences, both authorised and unauthorised. The final columns show the number of pupils in the school, the number of statements of special need and the number with special needs but without statements.

You could be forgiven for thinking that all this information would tell you what you want to know about a school's performance but this is not the case. What the tables do not show is the ability of the pupils on entry to the school. If, for example, we look at the Berkshire results in 1996, we find that Eton's pupils achieved a 96 per cent higher grade pass rate at GCSE higher grades while the comprehensive school next to it in the list achieved 61 per cent. Does this mean that Eton is better or worse than The Emmbrook mixed comprehensive school? All the tables tell us is how well the schools do with the pupils they happen to have. Many of the schools with low scores may well be offering a better education than schools with higher scores. In the coming years it is hoped to develop a more sophisticated ranking system which will show how much 'value' each school has added to the performance of the pupils it has in the school, i.e. have they improved at the same rate as the national norm, better or worse?

If raw comparisons with other schools are not helpful to parents, it may be worth looking in more detail at the results of the different departments within your children's school. If the school's overall results are average, i.e. about 45 per cent of Year 11 achieve five or more higher grades, you could expect the performance of each department to be about the national level for higher grades in that subject. The pass rates vary from subject to subject so you cannot compare Maths with Art without knowing what the national pass-rate is in each of the subjects and what the

135

school's exam entry policy is. A department which seems to be doing well may be achieving its success by only accepting the most able pupils into its teaching groups.

The topic of academic progress compared to national norms may be the kind of issue which you would consider raising at the PTA education forum referred to above. It is unwise to rush to conclusions about performance without specialist advice.

## Inspection by OFSTED

All state schools are inspected by teams of inspectors, including a lay inspector, on a six-yearly cycle (except for schools requiring special measures). The inspectors will watch a large number of classes and will look rigorously into all aspects of the school's life. They then prepare a report, a summary of which has to be sent to all parents, and the complete report has to be available for those who wish to read it. After the inspectors have reported, the Governors have to draw up an action plan which addresses the issues raised by the report. They then have to refer to the progress in meeting the targets laid out in the action plan at the next Annual Meeting.

Parents have an important part to play in the early stages of the process. You will be invited to attend a meeting with the leader of the inspection team, the Registered Inspector, at which nobody other than parents will be present. There will also be a questionnaire circulated to all parents and a summary of the responses to the questionnaire may be included in the final report.

All this gives you ample opportunity to let the Inspector know what you think about the school. Although there appears to be some expectation that you only turn up at the meeting or fill in the questionnaire if you have a complaint to make, it is just as important for you to make positive comments on the school so that the Inspector gets a balanced picture.

# *The school's finances*

Since 1988 all schools have had much greater responsibility for their own management, including finance. Local Management of Schools (LMS) has taken away many of the former controlling powers of the LEA and has transferred responsibility to the governing body of the individual school. In financial terms, this means that the school receives its budget as a lump sum and is free to spend it how it wishes. The Governors can choose to spend what they want on teachers, on books and equipment, on redecoration and maintenance of the buildings. Typically, 70 per cent of a secondary school's expenditure will be on the teaching staff, 7 per cent on non-teaching staff, 14 per cent on premises (rates, heating, lighting and maintenance), and 4 per cent on books and other learning resources.

Schools receive money in relation to the number and age of the pupils in the school. This is part of the competitive market-place in education which has been developed over recent years. The total amount of money which a school receives is determined by the amount given to local government by central government, with some marginal flexibility for decision-making at LEA level.

State schools today are working under severe constraints. The reduction in public funding for schools over the last few years has meant an increase in class sizes, the closure of teaching groups when too few pupils opt for a minority subject and a general shortage of text books and equipment.

Everything that happens in a school has to be paid for by the school. Damage to furniture, for example, means that less money will be available for text books. If your child wilfully damages school property, you may be sent a bill for its repair. Our advice would be that you warn your child very clearly about the importance of being careful and thoughtful in relation to school property.

Although state school education is basically free, i.e. provided through rates and taxes, schools can charge for certain activities and these will be laid out in the Charging and Remissions Policy in the school prospectus (see Chapter 2).

Such is the shortage of funds in many schools that your help may be sought in raising extra money. Parental fund-raising can be helpful in the provision of extra books and equipment. A typical annual spend on a secondary pupil's books and equipment is about £2 for each week of the school year so parental donations can make quite an impact in that area. Very few schools rely on parental funding for the payment of teaching staff.

If you have links with the commercial or industrial world, you may be able to help the school by looking out for any unwanted materials or equipment which could be of use to the school. You may also be able to put the school in touch with potential sponsors of school events or with advertisers for their publications.

# *Further reading*

**Becoming a school governor,** Department for Education and Employment. An introductory free booklet.

**Governors are people like you,** Joan Sallis, ACE, ISBN 1870672 45 3.

**Home and School: Partnership policies,** ACE in the 'My child in school' series.

**How schools work – a really simple guide for Governors and Parents,** ACE, ISBN 1 870672 10 0. If you are interested in knowing about school governance in more detail, you would benefit from reading this.

**How to complain,** Local Government Ombudsman (address in Appendix 12).

**Keeping Parents informed,** ACE in the 'My child in school' series.

**School governors' guide to the law,** Department for Education and Employment.

**Taking a few risks,** John Bastiani, Royal Society of Arts, 8 John Adam Street, London WC2N 6EZ, £12.50 plus £2.50 postage and packing. A useful book which looks at how teachers, parents and pupils could learn from each other.

**Taking matters further,** ACE in the 'My child in school' series.

# Useful organisations

**AGIT (Action for Governor Information and Training),** c/o Community Education Development Centre, Lyng Hall, Blackberry Lane, Coventry CV2 3JS. Tel: 01203 638679.

**National Association of Governors and Managers,** 21 Bennetts Hill, Birmingham B2 5QP. Tel: 0121 643 5787. It provides information and training for Governors. Governor training is also provided in some areas through the LEA.

**National Confederation of Parent Teacher Associations** is based at 2 Ebbsfleet Estate, Stonebridge Road, Gravesend, Kent DA11 9DZ and can provide practical advice on setting up a PTA. They also publish a quarterly magazine **Home and School** which helps to spread good practice in home–school relations.

**National Governors' Council,** Glebe House, Church Street, Crediton, Devon EX17 2AF. Tel: 01363 774377.

This body brings together LEA-based councils of Governors and is primarily a lobbying body on behalf of state schools.

**OFSTED (The Office for Standards in Education),** Alexander House, 29-33 Kingsway, London WC2B 6SF. Tel: 0171 421 6800. This body organises the inspection of schools across the country and issues general reports from time to time on the state of education.

**The Royal Society for the encouragement of Arts, Manufactures and Commerce (RSA),** 8 John Adam Street, London WC2N 6EZ. Tel: 0171 930 5115. The RSA has a project on Parents in a Learning Society and has produced the UK Directory of Home–School Initiatives, as well as other useful publications.

# CHAPTER SEVEN

# Life outside school and at home

During the secondary age years, the world outside school – life at home and in the community – start to exert a greater influence.

In this chapter we look at some aspects of adolescent development and their impact on school work:

- the expanding world of the adolescent
- relationships
- part-time jobs.

## *The expanding world of the adolescent*

The few years between the beginning of secondary education and the end of it are a time of rapid growth and development in the life of a young person. Starting in Year 7 as a mainly home-based, family-centred child, he or she will leave in Year 11, 12 or 13 as a young adult, physically stronger and personally more independent.

By that time, your children will have wider circles of friends and will be developing strong personal interests.

The teenage years get a bad press and everybody expects them to be difficult. It needs to be said that most young people do grow up successfully and that the vast majority maintain basically good relations with their parents. Although teenagers can do stupid and thoughtless things at times, most of them are caring and sensitive people who still need parental support more than they are prepared to admit.

There may well be clashes between the expanding world of social interests and the expectations of the narrow academic programme this book is mainly dealing with. Parents stand at the junction between those two worlds, simultaneously holding on to the demands of schoolwork and yet letting their children loose into the wider world.

## The changing relationship of parents and children

Although there are now many books of good advice on how to cope with teenagers, there is no one correct way for parents to relate to their teenage children. This is not only because all teenagers are individuals but also because they are not consistently the same throughout this period of their lives. There may be times with the same adolescent when quiet support is appropriate while at other times the same young person may need firmer guidance.

The basic advice from the experts amounts to the following guide-lines which are simple to write but less easy to live out in the real world:

- As parents you must recognise the need to let go.
  However strongly you feel the need to protect your
  children from the big bad world outside, they ultimately
  have to come to terms with it for themselves.

HELP YOUR CHILD THROUGH SECONDARY SCHOOL

- Keep the channels of communication open at all times, even when you are not getting much response from your teenagers. Do not pester them with questions, and do not lecture them, but be ready to listen to them when they want to talk.

- Even when they do things which hurt or upset you, keep your trust in them and they will eventually respond to your confidence in them. Keep on loving them as people even though you do not like some of the things they are doing.

- In terms of behaviour (fashion and clothing, going out, coming back late, seeing particular friends, etc.), do not seek to lay down the law and impose your conditions at any price. They do need to know what the rules are and what your expectations are, but it is better to arrive at those by a process of negotiation rather than imposition.

- Emphasise that you are above all concerned for their safety and well-being. Although they may want to go off in ways different from you at their age, recognise that they are themselves and not just clones of you. They are living in a different era and are subject to different pressures than those you knew at their age. For their own safety and for your own peace of mind, try to let them see that you need to know where they are going and when they will be coming back and how. If there is a change of arrangements, they must let you know.

- Keep a sense of perspective in your demands and expectations. Although you may find their untidy bedroom a deplorable example of thoughtlessness, keep reminding yourself that it is not the end of the world if they want to live in a pig-sty. After all, you were as bad as they were at that age and look at you now!

- If you are worried about your children, don't be embarrassed about seeking help from friends who have been through similar experiences or from all the agencies which now exist to support parents and adolescents. You may feel that the wayward nature of your children is a reflection on you and wish to hide your sense of guilt but it can help you to share your anxiety with others.

- One of your main worries will be the risks associated with drugs, solvent abuse and alcohol. We look at these in more detail in the next chapter. The use of illegal drugs of any kind cannot be ignored because they are potentially dangerous. Become well informed (taking professional advice if necessary), talk about the risks sensibly but frankly, try to find out what they have been using, talk through the reasons for their use of drugs and plan a way forward together. Remember that this is a common problem so share your concerns with whoever can help – school, police, youth service, social services – depending on the circumstances. Do not feel that you have to go it alone.

## Widening horizons

During the teenage years young people begin to relate more fully to groups and organisations outside the home. If they are to play a full part in adult life, they need to broaden their experience and yet you want them to do it in a safe and reasonably structured way.

There are a number of organisations – youth clubs, church groups, sports teams, special interest groups, the uniformed groups (Scouts, Guides, Boys Brigade), bands, orchestras, choirs, drama

HELP YOUR CHILD THROUGH SECONDARY SCHOOL

clubs – which are keen to recruit. You will be able to find a list of local addresses in your library. Our advice is to encourage your children to try joining in some of these structured activities, even though there may sometimes be a clash between school pressures (homework) and commitment to evening and weekend activities. The secret, once again, is time management.

The school holidays offer more opportunities for activities which will increase your child's independence but in a safe context. Schools offer trips and study visits; commercial companies have a wide range of adventure holidays which are advertised in national papers. All activity centres which offer outdoor pursuits involving any element of risk now have to be registered, inspected and accredited.

For older teenagers, it is possible to combine a holiday with community service, both in this country and abroad.

Many of the possibilities referred to above can be expensive. Less so are the holiday activities arranged in local schools during the summer where there are no residential costs because the children are coming back home each evening. These summer camps are well worth looking into, especially where you are out at work for part of the holidays.

If you can, consider letting your children take part in an exchange with a boy or girl from the country whose language they are learning. Apart from the journey cost and pocket money, this is a relatively cheap holiday because the visitor is treated as an extra member of the family. Exchange visits can be arranged through school, through private companies or through a national organisation. The value of such an exchange is that it not only improves your children's foreign language skills, but that it introduces them to another culture, another family and another way of thinking. Exchanges can of course involve the risk that the families may not be compatible but more often than not they are successful and in many cases, this can be the beginning of a contact which lasts a lifetime.

# *Relationships*

One of the most difficult aspects of adolescence for parents to come to terms with is the fact that their children are going to develop a much wider range of relationships with others. This is all a necessary part of the process of cutting the cord and moving into independence.

## Relationships with other adults

At this stage in their lives many teenagers will be coming into contact with a wider range of adults – teachers, leaders of clubs they belong to, sports coaches, church or youth group leaders, the people they work for. This will help them to develop the social skills which are the basis for future success and happiness. They will learn the importance of reliability and consistency in dealing with others. They will learn how to accept and give instructions. They will learn how to accept people they may not very much like at first. They may well feel attracted to some of the older people they meet and they will have to learn when it is appropriate to express their feelings and when not. They will learn that adults are fallible. This is an important aspect of becoming a mature individual.

Parents can help at this stage by encouraging teenagers to meet a wider range of adults and to talk about the people they are coming into contact with. Analysing relationships comes more easily to girls than to boys so you may need to make a greater effort with boys.

## Relationships with peers

For many teenagers, the first step out of the family nest is when they align themselves with a strong, closely-knit circle of friends. To be one of the gang matters deeply and parents need to respect this, even though they may not always approve of the people their teenagers are mixing with. Peer group pressure, i.e. the need to do something you would not otherwise have done because everybody is doing it, can be extremely powerful.

The role of the parent should be to take an interest in the circle of friends rather than being judgmental. You need to respect your children's right to have their own friends, not just ones you approve of. If you find that your teenagers are being drawn into activities with which they are personally uncomfortable (such as smoking, experimenting with drugs, behaving in a disruptive way in public), try to get them to talk through the tensions they are experiencing. Reassure them that if they decide to dissociate themselves from an activity of which they disapprove, i.e. if they resist peer-group pressure, they may gain in self-respect even if they fall out of favour with the group for a short time.

Young people who belong to ethnic minorities may experience additional tensions during adolescence in relation to their peer group. The wish to assert their personal independence may conflict with strong cultural messages about commitment to and respect for the family. Furthermore, in wanting to be accepted by his ethnic peer group, the child may be aware that this is not necessarily the same as acceptance by the wider adolescent world.

There can be a serious clash between the circles of friends within school and those outside and this can have a harmful effect on schoolwork. Typically a girl with a circle of older friends may find she is under pressure to devote less time to homework than her peers who may have left school already. All we have said in Chapter 4 about trying to negotiate a reasonable balance between work and leisure applies here, but under even more difficult circumstances.

Friendships outside school, particularly when they go wrong, can intrude into behaviour and concentration within school. This requires sensitive discussion – and try to explain to your child the fact that we all need, from time to time, to compartmentalise our lives and to put up mental barriers so that our effectiveness in our work is not diminished.

# Sexual relationships

Part of the widening of your teenager's circle of relationships will include a growing awareness of sexuality. Many parents find this difficult to come to terms with because it is such an obvious sign of their children's growing up as well as being a reminder that they themselves are ageing!

Surveys of teenagers show that they would prefer to receive information about sex from their parents (rather than from friends or other sources). However, many feel that their sex education is too little and too late and boys in particular are less well informed than girls. It is not essential to be able to answer every question. It is more important to show a willingness to talk and look for answers together.

The Trust for the Study of Adolescence has produced some excellent material to guide parents and several helpful books are listed at the end of this chapter. The main principles are:

- Make sure your teenagers have information to avoid unnecessary risk. You cannot assume that school has told them all they need to know. The science curriculum will covered the main biological aspects and in PSE they should be told about sexually transmitted diseases, AIDS and homosexuality (unless they have been withdrawn from these lessons at parental request). Some teachers are more effective than others in explaining the emotional pressures on teenagers and there is a big difference between talking about this in a PSE lesson and experiencing it for yourself, especially for the first time. If you have difficulty in talking about sex, make sure that there are booklets and pamphlets available (see the end of the chapter for further details).

- Be available to talk things over but don't get obsessed with the subject. Sooner or later you are going to have to trust your son or daughter to behave in a responsible way. The opportunities for constructive dialogue will probably arise unexpectedly rather than by being artificially created. Sitting down with a cup of tea to talk about the birds and the bees is no longer recommended practice. Newspapers, television programmes and magazines provide plenty of real-life examples which fall more naturally into family conversation.

- Help your teenagers not to feel pressurised into entering into a first sexual relationship until they know they are ready. Contrary to popular opinion, only a minority of young people (one in four in some areas and as few as one in eight in others) are sexually active before the age of 16. A good relationship should not depend on intercourse at too early a stage. However, if intercourse is going to happen, make sure that your children know about contraception. Boys in particular need to be aware of their responsibility towards their partner. Sexually transmitted diseases and pregnancy don't just happen to others.

- Do not feel guilty about your worries in relation to your teenager's sexual development. It is one of the most difficult aspects of parenthood. When a young person starts having a sexual relationship, it is a symbol of maturity, and when that happens to a person who in many other ways is immature, the tension for parents is painful. Sexuality is linked to identity and individuality, and an intimate relationship with someone outside the family is a statement of separateness. Mothers and fathers have to make a considerable adjustment to accept this change.

- Accept the situation even if you do not approve; keep listening and provide a shoulder to weep on; be willing to let them fly the nest.

LIFE OUTSIDE SCHOOL AND AT HOME

# *Part-time jobs*

Most teenagers look forward to taking up a part-time job in order to provide an independent source of income. As well as the financial benefits, part-time work can also give youngsters a sense of independence and responsibility, and provide a genuine experience of the world of work.

However, there are some potential disadvantages which you will need to watch out for, in addition to the obvious danger of your child becoming over-tired. Does the early morning job make for a late or rushed start for school? Does the evening job leave enough time and energy for homework? Does the job prevent her from following more interesting after-school activities? Is the work safe and suitable?

There are laws and bye-laws which control the employment of children and you can get advice about these from your local authority. For instance, you should be aware that:

- it is illegal for a child under 13 years old to work (except odd jobs or light agricultural / horticultural work for parents)
- children (see below for a definition) must not be employed doing heavy lifting or carrying
- it is illegal to work without a work permit
- children may not work in a factory or an industrial setting (e.g. factories, mines, transport or construction work)
- children must not work for more than two hours on a school day or Sunday. On school days they may only work between 7.00 am and 8.30 am, and between close of school and 7.00 pm.

The Department of Health is considering relaxing Sunday limits and will probably do so during 1997.

Other limits apply to Saturdays and during holidays, and vary according to age and local bye-laws. Appendix 7 provides an example of one local authority's time and age limits, but you will need to find out from your local Education Office about limits that apply in your area.

These requirements apply to children up to the end of compulsory school age. For children who turn 16 on 1st September to 31st January this is the beginning of the Easter holidays; for those who turn 16 on 1st February to 31st August, it is the Friday before the last Monday in May.

Local authority bye-laws also restrict the *types* of job children are allowed to do. For example, children may be prohibited from working:

- in the preparation of food in restaurants, pubs, fish and chip shops and hotel kitchens
- in serving alcoholic drinks in pubs, clubs and restaurants
- in cinemas, discos and theatres
- anywhere where gambling is allowed, such as clubs, amusement arcades and racetracks
- using dangerous machinery, or handling petrol or other dangerous substances.

Children are generally allowed to do the following sorts of work:

- in shops, such as stacking shelves or at the till
- delivering newspapers
- shampooing or sweeping up at a hairdresser's
- serving at table
- gardening
- office work
- car washing by hand.

One of the most popular jobs for teenagers is baby-sitting. A MORI poll in late 1996 showed that baby-sitting is undertaken by 40 per cent of children who work. This is an unregulated type of work which does not require a work permit. There is no legal age limit for baby-sitting; however, a sixteen-year-old is not yet an adult, therefore it is the parents employing the baby-sitter who would be responsible if anything happened to their child whilst in the care of a person under 16 years old. The parents could only take action against the baby-sitter if they could show that it was reasonable to leave their child with the person under 16, and that the baby-sitter did not exercise reasonable care.

Whatever job your child has, you might ask her a few discreet questions to check that her employers are being responsible and fair in the requirements and conditions of the job. Many employers are not aware of the law on young people and work. Some are simply exploiting young people as cheap labour.

Your child will need to apply for a permit before starting a part-time job. Forms are obtainable from the local authority and sometimes from the school. The employer has to fill in details of the hours and type of work. You will also need to sign it, as may your child's Headteacher. The local authority then checks all this before issuing a work permit.

# Further reading

**Adolescence: the survival guide for parents,** E Fenwick and T Smith, Dorling Kindersley, 1993.

**Coping with crushes,** Anita Naik, Sheldon Press, 1994, offers advice and help on how to cope with different types of crushes on famous people, teachers, girls, boys and people of the same and opposite sex.

**Is everybody doing it?** A guide to contraception, peer pressure and safer sex, published by the Family Planning Association (for address see page 153).

**Let's talk about sex,** Walker Books, London, provides thorough, frank, up-to-date and reassuring information about all aspects of growing up. Available from the Family Planning Association, for 10 to 14-year-olds, their parents and carers.

**Living with a teenager,** S Hayman, Piatkus, 1994. Insights and strategies to help parents understand teenagers' needs.

**Teenagers in the family,** Debi Roker and John Coleman, ISBN 0 340 62106 0 and **Teenagers and sexuality** ISBN 0 340 621052, John Coleman, both from Hodder and Stoughton in the Positive Parenting series, give plenty of information and advice which parents will appreciate. They are written by psychologists from the Trust for the Study of Adolescence. In conjunction with Carlton TV, the Trust has also produced a video and booklet called **Teenagers: a survival guide for parents** and this is available for £4.95 direct from Carlton TV, PO Box 101, London WC2N 4AW.

**When your child comes out,** A Lovell, Sheldon Press, 1995, helps parents come to terms with their feelings when their child tells them he or she is gay. Available from the Family Planning Association.

**Teenagers growing up in a Step-family,** Erica De'Ath (1990), STEPFAMILY publications, ISBN 1 873309 00 7, £1.20.

# Useful organisations

**The Brook Advisory Centre** provides contraceptive advice and counselling to teenagers and young people. It is free and confidential. To find the nearest centre, contact Central Office, Brook Advisory Centre, 165 Grays Inn Road, London WC1X 8UD. Tel: 0171 713 9000.

**Central Bureau for Educational Visits and Exchanges,** 10 Spring Gardens, London SW1A 2BN. Tel: 0171 389 4004.

**Community Service Volunteers,** 237 Pentonville Road, London N1 9NJ. Tel: 0171 278 6601. CSV works with youth groups, schools, colleges and universities to involve young people in positive community action, enabling people to play an active part in the life of their community in the UK and abroad.

**Exploring Parenthood** offers advice and counselling to parents on issues of family relationships and children's development and behaviour. Their advice line is open from 10.00 am to 4.00 pm on Monday to Friday on 0181 960 1678 and you can write to them at Latimer Advice Centre, 194 Farston Road, London W10 6TT.

**Families need Fathers,** 134 Curtain Road, London EC2A 3AR. Tel: 0171 613 5060. This is a national organisation for one-parent families, with local groups.

**Family Planning Association,** 2-12 Pentonville Road, London N1 9FP. Tel: 0171 837 5432. It has a series of publications entitled **Growing Up** which may help parents who have difficulty in talking about sex with their adolescent children, and a mail-order book service.

**GAP** provides opportunities for young people to experience work, travel or community service abroad during the year between school and university. Tel: 01734 894194.

**Gingerbread,** 16-17 Clerkenwell Close, Clerkenwell, London EC1R 0AA. Tel: 0171 336 8183. This is the national organisation for one-parent families; it has local groups.

**National AIDS Helpline,** open 24 hours a day. Tel: 0800 567123.

**The National Step-Family Association,** Chapel House, 18 Hatton Place, London EC1N 8RV. Tel: 0171 209 2460.

**Parentline** offers help and advice to parents on all aspects of bringing up young people. Their number is 01702 559900.

# CHAPTER EIGHT

# When things go wrong

Although we do not want to suggest that the adolescent years are inevitably troublesome, it is true that many young people and their parents will experience times of difficulty. This chapter has not been written to depress you but to forewarn you, to suggest how you will be able to manage and how you can find help if things start to go wrong.

These are the areas we will look at:

- school discipline
- behaviour problems
- school attendance
- alcohol, drugs and solvent abuse.

## *School discipline*

Since adolescence is the stage of asserting independence and testing the limits of authority, it is unlikely that your child will sail through secondary school without overstepping the mark at some time. Whilst we would not wish to suggest that your child is abnormal if he is always perfectly well behaved, you will be in the minority of parents!

A reasonable ambition is that, whatever your child does that gets him into trouble, it is not too serious, he learns from the experience and he doesn't do it again.

Discipline problems are a problem for the pupil, for the pupil's group and for the school. A pupil who messes around during lessons is putting obstacles in the way of his own learning, the learning of others and the efficient running of the school. The consequences go further than most pupils or parents see, including damage to teachers' self-esteem and professional confidence, and the invisible time costs of dealing with pupils referred out of lessons. It is important if your child misbehaves at school to recognise the ripple effects within the school.

Equally, though, you can expect to be treated as equal partners in resolving any problems, and not made to feel as if *you* were the naughty child.

Schools hope that parents will be supportive of any action they take in the event of misconduct, but you have a balancing act to perform between supporting the school (if you feel that they have acted reasonably) as well as helping your child cope with the message and any accompanying punishment.

As a general rule, avoid giving double punishments: if your child has been punished at school it is usually enough to register your disapproval of the behaviour without adding a punishment of your own.

Secondary schools generally have **behaviour policies** which describe, for example,

- their positive approach of encouraging, recognising and rewarding good behaviour
- their expectations and rules
- their policy on bullying, racial or sexual harassment
- the stages of their disciplinary procedure
- their sanctions for unacceptable behaviour
- the involvement of parents.

WHEN THINGS GO WRONG

A staged approach to disciplinary procedures involves a pupil being dealt with by different members of staff according to the seriousness of the misdemeanour, starting with the form tutor, then the Head of Year or Head of House, and at the most serious stages involving the Deputy Head and finally the Headteacher.

Verbal reprimands may be accompanied by a punishment according to the severity of the offence. Schools vary in the sanctions they apply but often include in their repertoire:

- missing breaks
- picking up litter (with appropriate health and safety precautions)
- conduct marks (which count against the pupil or pupil's group)
- extra work (few schools now regard 'lines' as a worthwhile punishment)
- after school or Saturday detention (following notification of parents; at present, schools cannot enforce detention if parents do not agree to it, but this may well change through future legislation)
- being put 'on report' (which involves being checked each lesson for good behaviour)
- exclusion from lesson(s)
- fixed term exclusion from school
- permanent exclusion from school.

Physical punishment in state schools is prohibited.

You can expect more serious or repeated offences to be accompanied by a letter or phone call home and a request for you to meet with the Year Head, Head of House, Deputy Head or Headteacher.

There are many good reasons for having a staged approach to dealing with unacceptable behaviour:

- to give pupils a clear understanding of the disciplinary consequences of their actions. This helps them to exercise self control

- to ensure that the punishment fits the crime. For example, a pupil who is cheeky receives a different response to one who is violent
- to 'nip problems in the bud', quickly and with a light touch. A simple warning may be all that is needed, rather than a formal punishment
- to allow different kinds and levels of misconduct to be dealt with by staff at the appropriate level, without having to take each incident to the highest authority
- to ensure consistency amongst staff, so that if a pupil is caught smoking by Mr B she receives the same response as she would from Mrs C
- to enable the school to develop a picture of a pupil's behaviour and to respond with helpful strategies in an organised way, calling in external help if necessary.

## Exclusion from school

An exclusion is when the Headteacher (and only the Head) decides that a pupil cannot come into school, either on a fixed term basis (up to 45 days in any year) or permanently. Permanent exclusion should only be used if allowing the child to remain in school would be seriously detrimental to the education and welfare of the pupil or others in the school.

Exclusion is a serious sanction since it involves missing opportunities for education. It should only be used as a last resort, for serious breaches of the school's discipline policy, and after proper investigation which includes the opportunity for the pupil to express a view.

The Department for Education and Employment (DfEE) recommends that exclusion is *not* an appropriate response to:

- breaking uniform rules for cultural, religious or financial reasons
- failure to complete homework
- non-attendance

- breaches of home–school agreements
- pregnancy.

Exclusion may be appropriate in cases of

- persistent bullying
- physical assault causing injury
- drug incidents (with distinctions between possession, consumption and dealing in illegal drugs)
- alcohol abuse
- use of a weapon to injure
- serious criminal offences, such as arson, sexual assault or grievous bodily harm.

Exclusion is often used following persistent disruption of lessons and seriously challenging behaviour.

Prior to the DfEE tightening up the law on exclusions in 1993, it was fairly common practice for schools to persuade parents to withdraw their child 'voluntarily' from the school in order to avoid formal exclusion. DfEE guidance makes it clear that this practice is unacceptable as it denies to the pupil and parents the safeguards of the formal exclusion process, including the right of appeal. Whilst transfer to another school can sometimes be an answer, do not let yourself be pressurised into removing your child from his school. If you do wish to transfer him, first of all secure a place at another school.

A question that parents often ask is whether a Headteacher can discipline a pupil for something that has happened off the school premises or outside school time. The answer to this is broadly 'yes'. For example, schools can make reasonable rules about behaviour on the way home from school (such as no smoking on the bus), and can apply sanctions for contravention of the rules. The actions of pupils outside school hours and premises can also result in disciplinary procedures when they have a serious impact on the life of the school. A hypothetical example is given below.

*Pupil A had a history of violence and intimidation towards other pupils and had received repeated warnings from staff. He threatened pupil B on several occasions whilst in school. He then assaulted and seriously injured pupil B on the way home from school. The Headteacher, after full investigation including interviews with the pupils and their parents, felt that the effect on pupil B was such that he could not resume his studies successfully if pupil A remained at the school. Moreover pupil A had failed to heed previous warnings about his aggressive behaviour. The Head therefore decided to exclude pupil A permanently.*

Before deciding to exclude a pupil, the Headteacher must take account of the individual circumstances of the case. For instance she must consider the pupil's age and health, previous record, domestic situation, and other influences (parents, friends) on the behaviour; she must also decide whether the offence affected other pupils, may recur, broke the school rules, involved others, whether it was on or off school premises, in or outside school hours.

It is also important that the school looks at whether the pupil has special educational needs which require a response beyond punishment for what he has done. This is quite a complex area, because the boundary between misbehaviour and having a behaviour problem which requires special help is not always clear. This is discussed further on pages 164–5.

## Fixed term exclusion

A fixed term exclusion can be from one to 45 school days in a year. If your child is excluded for a fixed term, the school should inform you of this on the same or following day. You should receive a letter telling you

- the length of the exclusion
- the reasons for it
- that you have the right to make representations to the governing body and to the LEA in an LEA school.

Many schools will also suggest a meeting with you to discuss the problem and tell you who else you can contact for advice and support, such as the local Education Welfare Officer.

If your child is excluded for more than five days or the exclusion would result in her missing a public exam, either the governing body or the LEA (in an LEA school) can direct the Head to reinstate her (allow her back). While your child is excluded for a fixed term, you can expect the school to provide her with work to do at home.

Fixed term exclusion procedures are the same in Aided schools as they are in LEA county and controlled schools. The LEA is not involved in exclusions from Grant Maintained schools.

Making representations means having an opportunity to put your views to a panel of Governors and/or to an LEA officer. You can do this even if the exclusion has already run its course, if you want to set the record straight. The school may agree to change aspects of your child's record. If not, you can ask for your views to be added. If you want to make representations you must write a letter to the Chair of Governors and/or the LEA to say so.

## Permanent exclusion

This is the most serious sanction of all. Sometimes pupils are excluded for a single offence if this is of a very serious nature, such as a serious assault on a pupil or teacher, drug dealing, arson or major theft. But more often, permanent exclusion is preceded by a build-up of poor behaviour, attempts to gain improvement, punishments and warnings and the involvement of parents.

If your child is permanently excluded, it is likely to be just as upsetting for you as him. It can be a time of uncertainty, anxiety, anger and shame. If you are on your own as a parent, find someone (a friend, relative, Education Welfare Officer, counsellor) with whom you can share what is going on, because no matter how reasonably and sensitively the school approaches this, the parents and pupil can feel very isolated and rejected.

You should hear from the school about the permanent exclusion as soon as possible after the Headteacher has made the decision. You should receive a letter giving you the same information as for a fixed term exclusion (see above) and also telling you:

- the date of a hearing (meeting) at which the Governors will consider the Headteacher's decision to permanently exclude
- details of previous disciplinary measures
- of your right to see a copy of your child's school record
- (if a Grant Maintained school), that you have the right of appeal to a committee of Governors.

## The exclusion hearing

Permanent exclusions are handled differently in County, Controlled and Maintained special schools, Aided schools and Grant Maintained schools. The procedures are explained in detail in Appendix 2. A brief summary is given below.

If your child is excluded from a County, Controlled or Maintained special school, the Governors *may* and the LEA *must* decide whether to confirm the exclusion or to reinstate him. In order to hear all the facts of the case a meeting is arranged at which the Governors' committee (usually three members), you and your child, and the Headteacher will be present. The LEA Officer may also attend that meeting rather than hear the case separately.

If the Governors decide to reinstate your child, he will return to school at a time specified by them. If the Governors confirm the exclusion, but the LEA decides to reinstate your child, he will return to school unless the Governors appeal to an independent committee against the LEA's decision. The Governors must do this within five days of the exclusion hearing. If both the Governors and the LEA confirm the exclusion, then you can appeal against this to an independent committee.

In Aided schools the LEA has no power to reinstate the pupil following a permanent exclusion. It is for a committee of the governing body to consider the case and either confirm the exclusion or direct the Head to reinstate the pupil.

Grant Maintained schools may adopt a similar procedure to County schools, except that the LEA will not be involved, and if the exclusion is confirmed by the Governors' disciplinary committee, any appeal will be to a second committee of Governors. However some schools do not invite parents to the initial Governors' disciplinary committee meeting. Instead, the Headteacher presents the case to the Governors' committee; if they confirm the exclusion they then inform the parents of their right of appeal to another committee of Governors. The parents are entitled to attend to present their case in person to the appeal committee.

The appeals procedures are described in Appendix 2.

## What happens next?

If your appeal is successful, the appeal committee will decide when your child should return to the school. You are, of course, entitled to transfer him to another school that has a place, if you prefer for him not to return. That is your decision and you should not feel any pressure to do so.

If your appeal is unsuccessful, arrangements must be made for your child's continuing education.

In many cases, excluded pupils transfer to another school. Legally, another school cannot refuse to take him if they have a place – i.e. if they have not reached the published admission limit for that year group (see Chapter 1, p20). Schools should not refuse to admit a child purely on the grounds of their behaviour or special educational needs. However, the reality is that schools vary in their willingness to give excluded pupils a second chance. Some schools are reluctant to take excluded pupils. Others are so accepting that they reach a point where to carry on doing so will jeopardise good order and balance within the school. You may need the help of an Education Welfare Officer or other LEA Officer to help you find a new school. Once accepted, it is very important that you give that school your full support in helping your child to settle and make a success of it.

In some cases, particularly with pupils who are nearing the end of their secondary education, it may be more appropriate for their education to continue otherwise than at a school. Most LEAs can draw on their own or external services in order to provide a satisfactory package of education, training and work experience for older pupils. The younger the pupil, the less appropriate it is for them to be outside a school setting. LEAs now have Pupil Referral Units which provide out of school education, sometimes on a short-term basis, whilst arrangements for re-integration to another school are being considered.

# Behaviour problems

Why do some children behave badly in school? There can be many causes. For example:

- boredom or difficulties with school work
- poor teaching, or teaching pitched at the wrong level
- unwillingness to accept rules and expectations
- inner emotional turmoil arising from things in or outside school
- desire for attention and low self-esteem
- medical conditions which affect behaviour.

Sometimes bad behaviour may be linked with learning difficulties which have not been identified, such as hearing or literacy problems.

There is a difference (although sometimes difficult to distinguish) between a pupil who sometimes does silly or unacceptable things and one who has behaviour difficulties. Pupils with long term or severe behaviour difficulties have a particular kind of special educational need. They require extra help and special strategies in order to get some improvement and gain fully from their schooling. The stages for the identification and assessment of pupils with special educational needs, described in Chapter 4 and Appendix 3, apply equally to pupils with behaviour difficulties.

The term *Emotional and/or Behavioural Difficulties* (EBD) describes a condition where the child is driven to disruptive, aggressive or anti-social behaviour, sometimes because they are unhappy or distressed.

Parents of well-behaved children often feel frustrated that their child's schooling may be affected by another child's disruptive behaviour. It may help to recognise that some of these children are having to cope with such a high level of personal stress and unhappiness that they cannot focus on school work or cope with school routines and expectations. If this is prolonged and shows little improvement such pupils may transfer to a special school for pupils with EBD.

Sometimes poor behaviour is caused by a medical problem affecting the functioning of the brain which prevents the child from following expected codes of behaviour. Well-publicised examples of this are the attention disorders: Attention Deficit Disorder (ADD), and Attention Deficit Hyperactivity Disorder (ADHD). Children with these conditions have very short attention spans, tend to be either attention-seeking or very disengaged, and do not respond to the normal tactics used by teachers to get pupils to settle, concentrate and behave themselves. ADHD has attracted much debate within the medical and education professions; there is controversy both about the diagnosis and its treatment with the drug, Ritalin.

Media attention on ADD and ADHD has caused some parents to leap to the conclusion that their child is a sufferer and that their problems will be solved by Ritalin. However, diagnosis is made by a medical officer, not by parents or the school. Where Ritalin is prescribed, this is usually as part of a broader therapeutic programme and parents as well as the school should be provided with full information about its usage and its limitations.

## What strategies do schools use to address persistently poor behaviour?

On a whole school level, one of the starting points for avoiding behaviour problems is to ensure that teaching is relevant, interesting and pitched appropriately to children's needs and abilities. Another key factor is the extent to which behaviour management is seen as a necessary element of professional development for all staff. Consistency of expectations and approaches in pupil–teacher relations is also an important baseline in establishing positive behaviour in a school.

In relation to individual pupils, you may hear teachers talking about a 'behaviour modification programme'. This refers to an organised approach to improving a child's behaviour. Sometimes a behaviour modification programme may be as simple as rewarding good behaviour and ignoring or minimising opportunities for unwanted behaviour. More often it will involve a number of different strategies such as target-setting, closer matching of work to ability level, making clear and simple requirements, agreeing a 'contract' with the child, offering responsibilities and rewards, and working with the child's strengths.

These approaches work best when the school has looked not only at the child but also at her environment, including the teaching. For instance, who does she work with best/least well? In what kinds of settings do positive and unwanted incidents occur?

The other essential ingredient for a successful behaviour modification programme is the parents' involvement. Children with behaviour problems need consistency in the expectations and responses of their significant adults. Working closely with the school also shows that you care, and that it matters.

### Early signs

How will you know if things are beginning to go wrong at school?

When a pattern of poor behaviour begins to develop, the school should pick this up and tell you about it. It is best addressed at the

### WHEN THINGS GO WRONG

earliest stage. You may also pick up the signs from things you notice or hear about at home, such as

- a negative attitude to and remarks about school
- frequent failure or reluctance to do homework
- a refusal or reluctance to conform with dress/uniform regulations
- frequent changes in friendships
- detentions or fixed term exclusions.

Not all of these, on their own, indicate a serious problem but you should try to find out what is behind the behaviour. Minor disaffection with school can lead to more challenging behaviour which in turn causes poor relationships with staff. This produces negative feedback to the pupil, which results in lower self-esteem and further disruption. It is a vicious circle which it is important to recognise and break.

Some types of behaviour have the potential to escalate from being relatively trivial to seriously challenging the school's authority. Uniform is a good example of this. Whatever individual staff and parents think about the principle of wearing uniform, if the school has a dress code, pupils will be expected to observe it. Children who continually test the boundaries by wearing non-regulation clothes find themselves in confrontations which unnecessarily create poor relationships with teachers. The school can use disciplinary measures (including exclusion) for persistent refusal to conform to reasonable and well-publicised rules about school dress, unless non-compliance is for religious or cultural reasons.

If you are worried about your child's behaviour at home, or suspect that she is developing a negative attitude to school, make early contact with her form tutor or Head of Year. This will reassure you either that the problem is not serious or that both you and the school can adopt a consistent approach and resolve it. You should also make regular contact to check on progress.

## What can parents do?

At the heart of many children's behaviour problems is low self-esteem. It is therefore important that in dealing with your child you emphasise that it is the behaviour you don't like, and not him. You don't hate him, you hate what he is doing.

As well as helping you to separate the child you love from the behaviour you dislike, this approach will help you to convey to him that you know he can behave differently. This is very important because if he thinks he is bad, he'll behave badly. If he thinks he can be good, he'll sometimes live up to that self-image.

Think about the language you use. Instead of saying 'You're a rude and unco-operative boy and I'm fed up with you' try 'It makes me feel angry/depressed/annoyed when you're rude to me and you don't do what I ask. Please will you . . .' In other words, describe the behaviour you don't like, the effect it has on you, and what you would like him to do instead. By saying how his behaviour makes you feel, you are emphasising the consequences of his behaviour, which will help him to feel some responsibility for his actions.

You should also try to catch your child doing good things and let him know you've noticed. Adolescents don't always respond to praise with warm gratitude – but your approval still matters to them. Sometimes, rather than praise, just describe the effect of their good behaviour: 'Thanks for tidying up. It made a big difference to come home and find you'd already done it.'

You can also:

- reward good behaviour and try to ignore unwanted behaviour (this is difficult!)
- check that your demands are reasonable and learn to compromise from time to time
- listen attentively and reflect back to him what you think he is saying. This not only shows that you are listening but also that you value and want to understand his views
- try not to let trivial things escalate into flaming rows. (You can

decide together in advance what you can do to stop a row in its tracks.) If things do escalate, try to explore (afterwards, when you've cooled down) what the issue really was.

There are many positive parenting approaches that can be learned, with plenty of books and videos now on the market. Some of these are described at the end of this chapter and Chapter 7.

## Who else can help?

Beyond the school there are a number of locally-based agencies who can help you and your child with behaviour problems.

- **Educational Psychologist** – contact is usually via the school. There are also psychologists who are independent of the LEA for whose services you would pay
- **Education Welfare Officer** – who can form a helpful link between you and the school, particularly in times of difficulty such as exclusion from school
- **Behaviour Support Services** in some LEAs
- **Home Tutors** – often employed when a pupil is out of school
- **Social Services**
- your **General Practitioner** – who may refer you to other services such as
- **Family Centre** (either run by Health or Social Services)
- **Child Psychiatry service.**

# *School attendance*

Just as with behaviour problems, there is a spectrum of attendance problems which ranges from being frequently late for school to persistent non-attendance. Both ends of the spectrum are a problem for the school in terms of disruption to lessons and time spent chasing up absentees, but even more of a problem is the effect on the child. National statistics show a clear link between consistent non-attendance at school, low achievement, later unemployment and anti-social behaviour.

If your child is regularly late for school he is disadvantaged in a number of ways. Over a year he is losing hours of schooling. He is probably missing key elements of the day, when instructions and messages are given. If he misses the introduction to a lesson he may never quite get the hang of it. He may be missing tutor group time which will affect his relationships with his tutor and peers. He is also failing to develop the essential work habit of good time-keeping which will be important in later life.

For all these reasons, if you are told by the school or the Education Welfare Officer (EWO) who works with the school that your child is often late, take it seriously. Try to identify whether it is because of poor time-keeping and organisation (does he have a watch?) or because he is getting up to something before going to school (stopping off in town, going to a friend's, having a smoke?). He will need a firm steer from you and back-up from the school. Lateness can also be a sign of disenchantment with school and can develop into truancy if not checked. It is therefore important to find out what is at the root of the problem. Your EWO can help you in this task. EWOs work with LEA and Grant Maintained schools.

Parents are legally bound to ensure that their child attends school regularly and to provide a note as soon as possible to explain any absences. You can be prosecuted by the LEA if your child persistently misses school. Before taking this course the EWO would work with you and your child to achieve regular attendance at school. As well as legal action the LEA can get an Education Supervision Order, which means that the court will appoint a supervisor to help you and your child towards full attendance.

Pupils' attendance is monitored by the school through morning and afternoon registration, as well as at each lesson. The EWO associated with the school checks registers and discusses individual cases with school staff. A difficult issue for schools is internal truanting, when a pupil turns up for registration but skips lessons. It is the responsibility of the school to address this problem by close monitoring and investigation of why it is happening. They will also need your support.

## Authorised and unauthorised absences

The various codes used in school registers indicate whether an absence is authorised or unauthorised. Schools follow DfEE guidelines in deciding whether absences fall into one or other category. Parents cannot authorise an absence. Some reasons for absence are acceptable, such as illness, medical or dental appointments, attendance at some religious events, or the death of a close relative. As long as the school receives a note giving these reasons, the child's absence will be marked as authorised. Other activities such as shopping for uniform or shoes, looking after younger siblings or helping you at home are not acceptable reasons for absence and will not be authorised by the school.

## Family holidays

Generally speaking it is not good for your child to miss school for a family holiday. There may be occasional cases where this is unavoidable, or would be educationally very valuable or where visiting family abroad requires a prolonged absence longer than the school holidays. The Headteacher (and not the parents) has the discretion to authorise up to ten days' family holiday during term-time, judged on the merits of the case. Authorisation is not automatic.

If you are going away for a long period (for example more than six weeks) you should check with the school or LEA that a place can be kept open for you. Policies on this vary. In an oversubscribed school, if your child's place is not left open you may have to appeal for re-admission.

# Alcohol, drugs and solvent abuse

There is a wide range of public attitudes towards the use of legal and illegal substances with harmful physical and social effects. The use by young people of alcohol, cigarettes, illegal drugs and solvents is causing concern but adult society is hypocritical and inconsistent in its response. For example, we preach the importance of not smoking yet allow the cigarette industry to continue to advertise its products.

Individuals have varying degrees of tolerance and acceptance: some would advocate strict prohibition and law enforcement; others, while recognising the dangers, wish to educate young people into behaviour which is socially acceptable and not harmful; some simply ignore the issue until a personal or family incident brings home to them the seriousness of lack of self-control.

The best general advice for parents is to make sure that their children understand:

- the physical dangers of consumption of harmful substances
- the laws surrounding their purchase and use
- the possible social consequences of their behaviour.

We have already looked in some detail at cigarette smoking in Chapter 5 so we concentrate here on alcohol and illegal drugs.

## Alcohol abuse

Alcohol is a drug like any other. The difference is that it is a legal substance. The similarity with illegal drugs is that it can have very harmful effects; it can cause death if a person overdoses on it.

Some of the health risks include:

- cirrhosis of the liver
- kidney failure

## WHEN THINGS GO WRONG

- memory loss
- cancer of the mouth, stomach or small intestine
- heart attack
- stomach ulcers.

As well as the health dangers, alcohol affects behaviour. It impairs judgement, leading to reckless or risky behaviour, which can result in accidents, trouble with the police or unprotected sex. Alcohol intensifies emotions; it can make you happy and gregarious, but it can also make you depressed and anxious.

It is important to ensure that your child is aware of the risks. You may not be able to stop her from trying alcohol; indeed, you may feel that this is part of growing up. However, you should try to discuss the dangers, and be alert to any signs of alcohol dependency.

Awareness of alcohol is increasing among younger children. The majority of eight-year-olds can recognise drunken behaviour in a film sequence and can sort bottles into alcoholic and non-alcoholic drinks. 10 per cent of 15-year-old boys drink more than 21 units of alcohol a week (a unit being defined as half a pint of beer, lager or cider, a single measure of spirits, a small glass of wine or sherry, or a measure of vermouth). The recommended weekly maxima are 21 units for adult men and 14 units for adult women, although even these figures are under revision. The difference between men and women is because the biological effect of alcohol differs according to the body weight of the drinker. Advertising affects the consumption of alcohol by young people and there is much concern about the influence of so-called alcopops, fizzy drinks with a low alcohol content.

Make sure your children are aware of the legal restrictions:

- It is an offence to sell alcohol (except with a meal) to anyone under 18.
- Children between five and 14 may not drink alcohol in any kind of licensed premises. They are only allowed in the bar of

licensed premises if it has a Children's Certificate and if they are accompanied by an adult. They are allowed in restaurants, family rooms and beer gardens provided that alcohol is not actually served there.

- Young people between 14 and 18 are allowed in bars at the licensee's discretion and may buy soft drinks and crisps, but they may not drink any kind of alcohol there. It is an offence to buy them alcoholic drinks, including shandy.
- Young people between 16 and 18 may buy, or have bought for them, beer, cider or perry (or, in Scotland only, wine) to drink with a meal, so long as it is consumed in a restaurant or area set apart exclusively for eating, and not in a bar.
- There is no law against the consumption of alcohol at home but a young person under 18 cannot purchase it.

Parents of teenagers are often concerned about the dangers of excessive drinking at parties in private homes. The obvious advice is:

- consume alcohol slowly and in moderation
- be aware that you might lose your inhibitions and find yourself in a situation with other risks (such as unprotected sex)
- make sure that any drivers drink absolutely no alcohol.

## Drug and solvent abuse

One of the sad but important differences between life when you were a child, and life for young people now, is the wide availability of illegal drugs and the high level of use by young people. It has been estimated that three out of five fifteen-year-olds have experimented with drugs.

This does not mean that three out of five are drug addicts (any more than you are an alcoholic because you enjoy the occasional drink). Many young people experiment with drugs but far fewer go on to develop a dependency on them.

It is not surprising, given this change in society and the sensationalist approach of the media, that parents can feel anxious and under-confident about how to approach this subject.

It is important to learn about drugs and solvents so that you can navigate this issue with your children and provide them with accurate information. At the end of this chapter you will find a list of helpful booklets and agencies.

Young people take drugs for a variety of reasons:

- to try out new and unknown things
- because their friends do it – a desire to conform
- as a way of gaining approval and self-esteem
- for the excitement and thrill of doing something dangerous or illegal
- for fun or relaxation
- to escape from problems or pressures
- as a way of challenging their parents
- because drugs are there and easy to get.

Possessing and supplying illegal drugs are criminal offences and punishable with fines or imprisonment. Although school pupils may not go to prison they will get a criminal record. Allowing drugs to be brought onto your premises is also a criminal offence.

## What sorts of drug are there?

The information booklets for parents suggested at the end of the chapter provide detailed descriptions and pictures of the variety of drugs and solvents which are available to young people. In Appendix 9 you will find a list of commonly used substances and their slang names (which are always changing!).

## How do I know if my child is using drugs?

It is not always easy for parents to know if their child is using drugs, partly because many of the signs are similar to those adolescents often exhibit. The Advisory Council on Alcohol and Drug Education (TACADE) suggests the following as possible signs of involvement in drugs:

- sudden changes of mood from happy and alert to sullen and moody
- unusual irritability or aggression
- loss of appetite
- loss of interest in hobbies, sport, school work or friends
- bouts of drowsiness or sleepiness
- increased evidence of telling lies or furtive behaviour
- unexplained loss of money or belongings from the home
- unusual smells, stains or marks on the body or clothes, or around the house
- unusual powders, tablets, capsules, scorched tinfoil, needles or syringes.

## What can I do as a parent?

You can minimise the risks of drugs to your children by opening up the subject so that you can explore the issues and provide information about the risks.

It is insufficient simply to instruct your children to 'say no to drugs'. This message on its own fails to recognise the complexity of the issues and the reasons for drug use amongst young people. Your message has to recognise that drugs are readily available and widely used; that some are very dangerous to health and others are risky, with unknown long-term effects; and that many legally obtainable substances are also dangerous. For instance, tobacco and alcohol cause more deaths and illnesses than illegal drugs. Legal solvents cause more deaths to youngsters than illegal drugs.

Although it is important for young people to be curious and to experiment, we have to provide them with the skills and knowledge to assess the risks of their behaviour. It's a difficult balancing act which is part of growing into adulthood.

As well as needing to know about the risks with drugs, your child needs to develop the confidence to resist peer pressure. The things you do to enhance his self-esteem will be very important:

- listen attentively and respectfully to his views
- show that you understand his point of view, even if you disagree with it
- talk to him; share your own views, feelings, fears and experiences
- be available, not at all times, but consistently
- let him know that you are there and that you care about him
- get to know his friends (without being intrusive) and if you can, let them have a place to meet together
- examine your own habits (for example over cigarettes or alcohol) and try to set an example
- try not to bully, scare or preach at him.

## What if I find my child is already using drugs?

Don't panic. Try not to overreact. If you are very angry or upset, do nothing until you have had a chance to calm down and you can think clearly. Hysteria is never a good starting point for dealing with this situation.

Once you have checked your facts you need to talk with him. Be calm and caring, but firm. Without disapproving of him as a person, you need to show your disapproval of using drugs. Give your reasons, including the facts that they can affect his health, and that they are illegal and could get him into trouble with the police.

If it was a one-off experiment with drugs, a talk may be all that is needed. If you suspect his involvement is greater than that, you may need help from outside.

Your doctor can offer advice on treating a drugs problem and there are also various agencies who can help in different ways. These are listed at the end of this chapter.

## What can schools do about young people's drugs misuse?

Drugs and solvent abuse is an issue for families and communities, and not just the responsibility of schools, but schools are in a good position to address this issue with pupils and their parents, and most do.

You should not assume that a school which goes public about the drugs issue has a problem with drugs. Schools which regularly provide drugs education for pupils and parents are acting responsibly and those who do not could be said to be letting their pupils down.

Schools usually provide drugs education through an organised programme within their Personal and Social Education (PSE) course. They often involve Drugs Advisory services who provide advice to staff and work directly with pupils.

The evidence does not suggest that teaching about drugs encourages experimentation amongst pupils.

As well as teaching them about the nature and dangers of drugs and solvents, schools will work with pupils on their social skills and self-confidence. The reason for this is that since we cannot stop the supply of drugs, we must help pupils to resist their influence. Happy, confident youngsters who have hobbies and interests and who feel good about themselves will have stronger defences against negative peer group pressures.

Schools can also provide a source of adult advice for pupils who feel at risk and need someone outside the family to talk to. Some schools will refer pupils to specialist agencies for advice. Teachers cannot guarantee confidentiality to a pupil who discloses that he is taking drugs.

## Drug-related incidents in school

No matter how conscientious a school is in educating pupils about drugs, there will be some who experiment with illegal drugs and harmful substances, sometimes on school premises.

Schools should have clear policies for dealing with drug-related incidents. These should address the disciplinary measures (for instance, should pupils be excluded?) the medical issues (being aware and ready to respond to pupil's immediate medical need), and the need for counselling and follow-up support for pupils.

Headteachers retain the responsibility for deciding on how a particular drugs incident in school should be dealt with. The fact that a pupil has broken the law does not of itself mean automatic exclusion from school. Within the framework of the school's policy, cases should be considered taking into account all the circumstances. The DfEE recommends that distinctions should be made to reflect the increasing severity of the offence: possession may be regarded as less serious than consumption; dealing in drugs is generally regarded with the greatest seriousness. Many schools will respond with a temporary exclusion for a first offence of taking drugs in school, whilst dealing could result in permanent exclusion.

In addition to learning about the health hazards, it is essential that your child is aware (through the school and you) that involvement in drugs can lead to exclusion, which could seriously damage his education.

# Further reading

### Drugs, alcohol and solvent abuse

**Exclusion from school,** a pamphlet produced by ACE, 1996.

**School attendance: information for parents,** Department for Education and Employment, 1995.

**A lot of bottle,** Derek Rutherford, Institute of Alcohol Studies, 12 Caxton Street, London SW1H 0DS. ISBN 1 871195 01 2.

**Drugs and your child,** a more detailed version of the booklet below, £1.50 from ISDD, 1 Hatton Place, London EC1 8ND.

**Drugs – a parent's guide,** and **Solvents – a parent's guide,** free, Health Publications, Unit Heywood Stores, No. 2 Site, Manchester Road, Heywood, Lancashire OL10 2PZ.

**That's the limit – a guide to sensible drinking,** Health Education Authority, Hamilton House, Mabledon Place, London WC1H 9TX.

# Useful organisations

## Drugs, solvent and alcohol abuse

**ADFAM National,** a charity for families and friends of drug users. National Helpline: 0171 638 3700.

**Families Anonymous**, a self-help support group with regional branches for parents of drug users. Tel: 0171 498 4680.

**The National Drugs Helpline** on 0800 77 66 00 is a 24-hour free helpline and can give you advice on how to talk to your child about drugs, confidential counselling or any other information on drugs. They will also give you details of support services in your area and how to make contact.

**Release,** Advice line: 0171 729 9904 during office hours and 0171 603 8654 at other times. Drugs in School (24-hour) Helpline: 0171 603 8654.

**Re-Solv (Society for the Prevention of Solvent and Volatile Substance Abuse),** produces leaflets, booklets and videos, and has information on local agencies who can help. 30A High Street, Stone, Staffs. ST15 8AW. Tel: 01785 817885.

**SCODA (Standing Conference on Drug Abuse)** provides information about where to go for specialist help. Tel: 0171 928 9500.

**TACADE (The Advisory Council on Alcohol and Drug Education),** 1 Hulme Place, The Crescent, Salford M5 4QA. Tel: 0161 745 8925.

## Parenting

**Exploring Parenthood: The National Parenting Development Centre,** provides an advice line for parents on 0171 221 6681; also runs training courses and produces fact sheets on common parenting issues: 0171 221 4471.

**The Family Caring Trust**, 44 Rathfriland Road, Newry, Co Down BT34 1LD. Tel: 01693 64174. Locally-based, parent-led courses in approaches to parenting. Also useful materials on parenting adolescents.

**Parent Network,** Room 2, Winchester House, Kennington Park, 11 Cranmer Road, London SW9 6EJ. Tel: 0171 735 1214; fax: 0171 735 4692. Organises training for parents to run Parent-Link courses on a local basis.

# CHAPTER NINE

# Support for parents

In the preceding chapters we've looked at how you as a parent can help your children get the most out of their secondary years. We have indicated the various ways that you can expect the school to support you, such as providing you with regular and clear information about how your child is getting on, creating opportunities for you to learn about the curriculum and educational matters, and making it easy for you to raise issues and feed back to them on the things that concern you or your child.

Beyond the school there are other agencies who will be able to help you in particular ways; some have been suggested in previous chapters.

The extra help available falls into two main categories:

- personal support
- financial support.

# *Personal support*

## The Education Welfare Service

You may have heard of the Education Welfare Officer (EWO, sometimes called Education Social Worker) while your child was in primary school. EWOs are employed by the Local Education Authority. Their main role is to ensure pupils' regular attendance at school and to work with parents, pupils and the school when there are problems with attendance. EWOs are also concerned with wider pupil welfare issues.

Each school usually has an EWO who visits regularly to check attendance registers and discuss individual problems and general issues with pastoral staff. EWOs also visit families to give advice and support where children are not getting to school regularly. They also provide information on welfare benefits, allowances and grants.

EWOs often provide a helpful link between parents and other agencies. For instance they can be supportive to parents when a child has been excluded from school, is in trouble with the police, or when family illness or breakdown create difficulties with schooling.

## Multicultural support services

In most authorities there are services available to help Traveller children and pupils for whom English is not a first language to get the most out of their education. Such services may provide second language support in classrooms, bilingual parent liaison officers and Traveller liaison workers. You can find out what help is available to you by asking at the school or by contacting your LEA.

## Special needs services

If your child has special educational needs, contact with specialist services is usually via the school. If your child has a Statement of Special Educational Needs or is undergoing Statutory Assessment you should have a named person who will provide you with information, support and advice (see Chapter 4).

## LEA Education Officers

Most education authorities have officers whose responsibilities include supporting and advising parents on specific and general issues relating to LEA schools. You can find out who to speak to by telephoning your local education authority office. General information about Grant Maintained schools can be obtained from the Grant Maintained Schools Foundation (for address, see Chapter 1).

## Citizens Advice Bureaux

Your local CAB will be able to give you advice on a range of legal and general issues relating to education. Their service is free, confidential and impartial. They can also provide information on welfare benefits, local services, family law and the rights of children. They will not normally intervene in matters related to school but will give you all the information and guidance you may need to resolve a problem for yourself.

## Social Services

The Social Services Department of your local authority supports and does preventative work with families with extreme difficulties, particularly where children may be at risk of harm or of being taken into care. Many Social Services Departments run Family Centres where different activities and groups are held to help parents and children experiencing problems.

## Health Authority

Under the umbrella of the Health Authority and local Health Services Trusts there are many services for families including Family Consultation, Child Psychiatry and Health Promotion services. Your GP should be able to advise you about these.

## National organisations which support parents

There are now many national organisations (some with local offices or groups) which provide support, guidance and information for parents. Some focus on specific aspects of parenting (such as the Sex Education Forum) or particular groups of parents (such as Gingerbread and Families Need Fathers for single-parent families); others cover a whole range of issues which concern parents. **We have listed these and other organisations at the end of each chapter where relevant.**

# *Financial support*

## Financial support from the education authority

Local education authorities can assist parents with certain school expenses if they receive Income Support or are on a very low income. For example:

### *Free school meals*

All school children under 19 years old whose parents receive Income Support (or who receive it themselves) can have a free daily school meal.

### *School clothing*

Secondary pupils who are still of compulsory school age (see page 150) and whose parents receive Income Support may be eligible for a grant towards clothing which is essential for school.

### *Education Maintenance Allowance*

This allowance is for students who are *over* compulsory school age and were under 19 years old at the beginning of the school year, and whose parents (or the pupil) receive Income Support.

This money is to help with books, equipment and course materials.

To claim any of these benefits you need to provide proof of your income and any state benefits you receive.

## *Assistance with transport*

Your LEA is obliged by the 1944 Education Act to provide free transport for eight to 16-year-olds living more than three miles away from their nearest school, whether it is an LEA or Grant Maintained school. The distance measured is the shortest available route which is safe for an accompanied child.

Most LEAs also provide assistance for students over 16 years old; this may be subsidised rather than free, since it is a discretionary service. Similarly, each education authority has its own policy for assisting with transport to denominational schools. Details will be available from the local Education Office or from the school.

## Other financial support for families

There are various government benefits of which you are probably, by now, aware. These are summarised below. Apart from some incapacity benefits, none of the following benefits depend on your National Insurance contributions. Detailed advice on these and other government benefits is available from your local Benefits Agency (formerly known as the DSS) Office, or from your local Citizens Advice Bureau.

## *Child Benefit*

This is a tax-free weekly benefit for nearly anyone who is responsible for a child. You can get Child Benefit for each child under 16. For children aged 16,17 or 18 you can get Child Benefit if the child is still in full-time education, up to and including A Level or its equivalent.

## *Income Support*

This benefit is to help people aged 18 and over whose income and capital are below certain levels and who are not working 16 hours a week or more.

## *Family Credit*

This provides a tax-free benefit for working families with children. It is not a loan and does not have to be paid back. You must be responsible for at least one child under 16, or under 19 if in full-time education up to and including A Level or its equivalent.

## *Housing Benefit*

This is available in certain cases of hardship and is paid by local councils to people who need help with their rent. Help with mortgage interest may be available if you get income support.

## *The Social Fund*

This fund, which has limited money available, helps people with expenses which are difficult to meet out of their regular income, for example items for a new baby, heating costs in very cold weather, or funeral costs.

## *Disability and incapacity benefits*

There are various allowances for people with disabilities or who are incapacitated through illness.

# Conclusion

If you have at last reached this part of the book, you may be for-given for thinking that helping your child through secondary school is an assault-course of increasing severity. We have inevitably looked at the problems and difficulties which may arise but we want to end by reassuring you that the vast majority of young people enjoy their secondary schooling, do well and turn out to be caring and compassionate adults. Despite moments of worry and frustration, the majority of parents enjoy seeing their children grow up and sharing in their successes.

As we have shown throughout this book, the guidance and sup-port available for parents and young people is greater than ever before. Do not be afraid to read widely, to ask for help and to share any concerns you may have with others.

Parents today are faced with difficult personal decisions:

- how much time should I make available for my children?
- should I/we both work full-time?
- how much should I 'interfere' with my child's education?

Your decision will be a compromise between all the pressures on you. We hope that this book will have enabled you to realise that what you continue to do for and with your children as they grow up is crucial to their long-term success.

If there is a single message to leave with you, it is this:

**Parents make a difference!**

# Admission appeals procedures

If your child is not offered a place at the school you prefer, you have the right to appeal to an independent appeals committee set up by the LEA, or in the case of GM and Aided schools to a committee set up by the Governing Body.

Not all parents appeal. Those who appeal usually do so because they feel that they have a particularly strong case. For instance:

- they may live within the catchment area of the school
- they may have another child already at the school
- their child's best friends may all be going to that school
- their child may have a special need or medical condition which makes that school more desirable
- there may be special family circumstances which are affected by which school the child attends
- they want their child to go to a single sex or denominational school.

Your reasons do not have to correspond to the admissions criteria of the school. The appeals panel will listen to any reasons you describe. The strongest reasons are often those which relate directly to your child's needs and welfare.

Many education authorities offer parents who wish to appeal the opportunity for an informal discussion with an Education Officer. This allows the Officer to describe the appeal process, to give background on the situation at the school, and to advise parents on their appeal.

## How to appeal

You will need to write a letter of appeal. Some LEAs provide a form with space for you to set out your reasons for appealing. If you do not have a form you could use the format below:

> *John Someone*
> *11 Somewhere Street*
> *Anytown*
> *Anycounty*
> *AB1 2CD*
> *0123 456789*
>
> *Child's name: Joanna Someone*
> *Date of birth: 1 January 1989*
> *Present School: Anytown County Primary*
> *Year 6*
>
> *To the Appeals Committee*
> *I wish to appeal against the LEA's decision (or Governors' decision for Aided or GM schools) not to allocate a place for my child [name of child] at [name of school].*
> *My reasons are . . .*
>
> *I attach the following documents which support my appeal*
> *. . . (e.g. a doctor's letter)*

You should send this to the address given on the letter you received about the allocation of a school for your child. That letter might also give you a date by which you should appeal.

You will receive a letter from the local authority (or the GM or Aided school) giving you a date for hearing your appeal, with at least fourteen days' notice. You will be invited to attend the appeal hearing. Although you do not have to be there, it is very much better if you are, so that you can explain your case fully and answer any questions.

You should also receive a statement from the LEA or GM/Aided school at least a week before the appeal date, setting out the reasons for not allocating your child a place.

Separate hearings may be held for each parental appeal, or, in some cases, hearings related to one school may be held together. If they are grouped you have the right to object to your case being heard in the presence of others.

The idea of attending a hearing may seem very daunting - but remember that you are not on trial! This is your opportunity to state your case. You are entitled to bring a friend, and this may help if you are nervous. Legal representation is allowed, but not usual, because as far as possible appeals are kept informal. Children do not usually attend, although there is nothing legally to prevent this.

## Who is on the appeals committee?

The appeals committee for *County and Controlled schools* will be made up of three (or sometimes five or seven) perfectly ordinary people! It will include:

- a lay person, who is not involved in the running of a school or education (except perhaps in a voluntary capacity)
- a member of the local authority
- a person 'experienced in education' (such as a retired teacher) who is not a member of the LEA

No member of the committee should have any direct involvement in or connection with the school for which you are appealing. The committee is set up so that it can take an independent view of your case. The Chairman must not be a member of the LEA and LEA members must not be in the majority.

Appeals committees for *Grant Maintained schools* are set up by the governing body and must also consist of three, five or seven members. These members must include:

- persons who are independent of the governing body who have experience in education, or are familiar with local education conditions, or are parents at another state school in the area
- a lay person who is independent of the Governing Body

and may include

- members of the governing body (who are not on the school's admissions committee).

The independent persons must not be employees or parents of pupils at the school. The governing body members must not outnumber the independent persons by more than one. The chairman of the appeals committee must not be one of the governing body members.

Appeals committees for *Aided schools* must again consist of three, five or seven people. The committee must include:

- a lay member
- persons from a list drawn up by the LEA

and may include

- members of the governing body (who have not been involved in the school's admissions decisions).

Governing body members must not be in the majority or chair the committee. A teacher at the school cannot be on its appeals committee.

## What does the appeals committee do?

The committee will listen to your reasons for wanting a place at the school and ask you questions. It will listen to the LEA's reasons for not offering you a place (or the Headteacher's or admissions committee's reasons in an Aided or GM school) and ask the Officer questions. It must then decide whether or not to allocate a place for your child. You also have a chance to ask and answer questions.

The committee has to decide whether the admission of any more pupils would lessen the quality of education provided at the school, or waste resources. The legal jargon is whether admission of your child 'prejudice the provision of efficient education or the efficient use of resources'. If the committee feels that the answer to this is 'yes', they may *still* decide to offer you a place if they think that your case outweighs the problems for the school.

The committee's decision is binding on the school and the LEA. You should receive the decision, in writing, shortly after the hearing.

## What if I am not successful in my appeal?

This is usually the point at which you accept that you have not got a place at the school.

However, most LEAs would allow a second appeal if there was a *significant* change in your circumstances (such as moving into the catchment area).

If you feel that the way the appeal was conducted was unfair or incorrect, you can complain to the Local Government Ombudsman (address from your local Citizens Advice Bureau). Although the Ombudsman cannot offer you a place, he or she can order that the appeal should be held again.

If you feel that the committee was not properly constituted (for instance, that there were too many LEA or Governor members), or that the LEA or Governors have not acted reasonably in carrying out their responsibilities, you can complain to the Secretary of State at the Department for Education and Employment (address in Appendix 12). The Secretary of State cannot review the decisions of individual appeal committees, but can direct the LEA or governing body to reconstitute the appeals committee.

If your complaint is taken up and investigated fully, be prepared for a long wait and further uncertainty.

# Exclusion hearings and appeals

## The exclusion hearing

Permanent exclusions are handled differently in Aided and Grant Maintained schools from County, Controlled and Maintained special schools.

If your child is excluded from a County, Controlled or Maintained special school, the Governors *may* and the LEA *must* decide whether to confirm the exclusion or to reinstate him. In order to hear all the facts of the case a meeting is arranged at which the Headteacher will present the case for exclusion to a Governors' committee (generally three members). You (and usually your child) will be invited to attend. The LEA Officer may also attend that meeting rather than hear the case separately.

You are entitled to bring a friend to the meeting. This person could be a solicitor but more often it is someone you know who can provide moral support and help you to present your case.

The Headteacher will describe the background and give her reasons for excluding your child. The Governors, you and LEA Officer can ask questions of the Head to get a complete picture. You will then have an opportunity to present your views and any further information, and if you do not think the exclusion is fair, to argue for your child to be reinstated. The pupil is generally also allowed to contribute and answer questions.

Once the facts of the case have been heard, you and the school withdraw from the meeting in order for the Governors and the LEA to come to their separate decisions. The Governors must let you know their decision within 15 days of the Head's letter notifying you of the exclusion.

If the Governors decide to reinstate your child, he will return to school at a time specified by them. If the Governors confirm the exclusion, but the LEA decides to reinstate, your child will return to school unless the Governors appeal to an independent committee. They must do this within five days of hearing the decision.

If the Governors and then the LEA confirm the exclusion, the LEA must let you know this within 20 school days of the Head's letter notifying you of the exclusion. You can appeal against this to an independent committee; you have 15 school days in which to write to the LEA saying that you wish to appeal. They must arrange a hearing within 15 school days unless you want more time.

In Aided schools the LEA has no power to reinstate the pupil following a permanent exclusion. It is for a committee of the governing body to consider the case and either confirm the exclusion or reinstate the pupil. The Governors must inform you of your right to appeal to an independent committee, within 15 days.

Grant Maintained (GM) schools may adopt a similar procedure to County, Controlled and Maintained special schools but the LEA will not be involved, and any appeal will be to an appeal committee composed of Governors and independent persons. However some GM schools do not hold the initial hearing with parents. Instead, the Headteacher presents the case to the Governors' discipline committee. If this committee confirms the exclusion they then inform you of your right to appeal to a second committee composed of Governors and independent persons. You have 15 school days in which to appeal. You are entitled to attend the appeal hearing to present your case in person.

# Appealing against permanent exclusion

Most of the principles and procedures of admission appeals described in Appendix 1 also apply to exclusion appeals, such as:

- the different composition of appeals committees for County, Controlled and Maintained special schools; and Aided schools, and Grant Maintained schools (see pp191–2)
- the opportunity for all parties to present their views, ask questions and answer questions
- the fact that the appeals committee's decision is binding
- your recourse to the Local Government Ombudsman or the Secretary of State if you feel that things have not been done properly or fairly.

In County, Controlled and Maintained special schools your appeal is against the LEA's decision to uphold the school's exclusion. In Aided and GM schools your appeal is against the decision of the governing body (represented by the discipline committee) to uphold the exclusion.

The procedure at an exclusion appeal is likely to be like this:

- the LEA or governing body case is presented, calling witnesses as necessary, (for example, the Headteacher)
- the parent asks questions
- the committee asks questions
- the parent's case is presented, calling witnesses as necessary
- the LEA asks questions
- the committee asks questions
- summing up by the LEA
- summing up by the parents
- the LEA and parent withdraw to allow the committee to consider
  - whether the pupil was responsible for the behaviour complained of
  - if so, whether it was reasonable for the Headteacher to respond with permanent exclusion

The appeal committee will normally let you know of their decision within two days of the appeal hearing.

# Special educational needs assessment process

## The stages of identification and assessment of special educational needs

The following stages are recommended in the DfEE Code of Practice:

### Stage 1

- Your child's teacher will record any concerns she has about your child's learning. The teacher or the SENCO (Special Educational Needs Co-ordinator) will discuss the concerns with you, tell you what measures the school will take and suggest ways in which you can help.
- Often this early help will mean that the problem is overcome.

### Stage 2

- The SENCO will talk with you and your child's teacher and the school will draw up an Individual Education Plan (IEP). This plan will include targets for your child and a date when progress will be reviewed. Your involvement and encouragement will continue to be important.

## Stage 3

- The school may seek external specialist advice, for example, from an educational psychologist or specialist teacher. Using this advice a new IEP will be drawn up which describes your child's difficulties and sets out an action plan to address them. You will be kept informed of progress and invited to review meetings.
- If satisfactory progress is not made the school will consider whether a Statutory Assessment is needed. You will be consulted about this.

## Stage 4

- The LEA will consider whether Statutory Assessment is necessary, and if so will gather detailed information on your child's needs from you and all relevant persons.

## Stage 5

- The LEA may decide to produce a *Statement of Special Educational Needs.*
- Alternatively, if the LEA thinks that your child's needs can be met by the school with its available staff, equipment and resources, a *Note in Lieu* will be sent to you. You should receive copies of all the reports on your child and be given reasons for the decision not to produce a Statement.
- If the LEA decides to produce a Statement, it is first produced in draft form. You (and others involved) have the opportunity to comment on it.
- Once the final Statement is issued, the LEA and school must provide the special help or facilities that are set out in it.
- The Statement will be reviewed at least annually and you will be invited to take part in each review meeting.

# Special Educational Needs Tribunal

The Special Educational Needs (SEN) Tribunal exists to provide an independent forum where parental appeals against decisions of the LEA can be considered.

## You can appeal to the Tribunal against

- the LEA's decision not to make a Statutory Assessment of your child's needs
- the LEA's decision not to issue a Statement after Statutory Assessment
- the description in your child's Statement of her special educational needs
- the description in your child's Statement of the special educational help that she should get
- the school named in her Statement
- the LEA not naming a school
- the LEA's refusal to change the school named in the Statement
- the LEA's refusal to re-assess your child's needs if they have not done so for six months
- the LEA's decision not to maintain the Statement.

## You cannot appeal to the Tribunal against

- the way the LEA carried out the assessment or the time it took
- the way the LEA is arranging to provide the help set out in the Statement
- the way the school is meeting your child's needs
- the description of your child's non-educational needs or how the LEA plans to meet those needs.

If you are unhappy about the issues above and cannot reach agreement through discussion with the school or LEA, you can complain to the Secretary of State that the school or LEA is acting unreasonably or failing to carry out its duties.

## You can get advice and help with an appeal from

- your Named Person (see p91)
- a voluntary organisation which helps people with your child's particular disability
- a parents' group
- a Parent Partnership Adviser within the LEA
- a solicitor (lists are available from the Citizens Advice Bureau).

The Department for Education and Employment (DfEE) booklet *Special Educational Needs Tribunal: how to appeal* gives clear information and provides many useful contacts for support and information. Copies are available from the DfEE Publications Department, PO Box 2193, London E15 2EU. Tel: 0181 533 2000.

# Parents' legal rights and responsibilities

The law presumes that parents have general responsibilities towards their children. In particular, parents are responsible for

- care and control of their children to a reasonable standard and ensuring that they do not suffer significant harm (under the Children Act 1989)
- ensuring regular attendance at school until sixteen (under the Education Act 1944)
- the financial maintenance and accommodation of their children until they reach eighteen or marry (under the Child Support Act 1991 and the Social Security Act 1986).

## When children get into trouble

If your child fails to act with reasonable care and hurts someone or causes damage, you are not liable for his negligence. However, parents are liable for their own negligence if they have not taken reasonable care to prevent their child from harming others. Parents are not legally responsible for offences committed by their child, but if your child is fined by the Court you may be expected to pay the fine.

# What is 'parental responsibility' in law, and who has it?

*Parental responsibility* as a legal term is defined by the Children Act 1989 as all the rights, powers, duties, responsibilities and authority which by law a parent of a child has in relation to the child and his/her property.

If the mother and father were married at the time of the child's birth or have married since, both have parental responsibility for the child. If they were not and have not married, then only the mother has parental responsibility. An unmarried father can acquire parental responsibility by

- obtaining a Parental Responsibility Order
- formal agreement with the mother, filed through a local Registry
- being granted a Residence Order by the Court
- being appointed a Guardian.

Step-parents, foster carers and grandparents do *not* have parental responsibility unless they have acquired it through a Court order. Although they are parents in the general sense, they do not have the legal authority to take important decisions about the child, such as which school she should attend (even though they might be very involved in the decision making).

## Section 8 Orders

Section 8 Orders (under the Children Act 1989) are Court orders which settle aspects of a child's care or upbringing when there is disagreement. They relate to what were known as *custody* and *access* issues. A Section 8 Order can specify one of the following:

- a **Residence Order** which says where and with whom the child will live
- a **Contact Order** which says who can have contact with the child

- a **Prohibited Steps Order** which prohibits named persons who have parental responsibility from specified actions
- a **Specific Issue Order** which requires the person to do what the order specifies (such as arrange visits to brothers and sisters or attend a particular school).

## Children 'divorcing' their parents

Children cannot 'divorce' their parents. Parents retain parental responsibility for their children (except after adoption) up to the child's eighteenth birthday. However, children can apply to the Courts for a Section 8 order to limit the responsibility and actions of their parents. This could include an order which allowed them to live with someone else.

## Changing a child's name

There are a number of circumstances in which parents may want to change their child's name, a common one being when a mother remarries and wants her children to take on her new married name. Most schools will rightly treat with great care any request to change a child's name in their records and general usage. Although, strictly speaking, one parent can change a child's name, another parent could object to this and then the parents would have to resolve the matter in the Courts. Many schools will therefore ask for the written permission of all those who have parental responsibility for the child (and the child herself), before they will make such a change. If the child is subject to a Care Order or Residence Order (see above) then it is illegal to change the child's name without the written consent of all those with parental responsibility or without leave of the Court.

## Taking part in school elections and ballots

If you do not have parental responsibility in the sense defined above but you are a parent in the practical sense of the word (i.e.

you live with and look after the child) you *are* entitled to take part in the election of parent Governors and to vote in a ballot about Grant Maintained status for your child's school. You are also entitled to see your child's records (with certain restrictions), to receive reports on his progress and to attend parent interviews.

## Divorced and separated parents

Whether or not you are living with your child, you are entitled to be involved in her education as long as you have 'parental responsibility' (as defined earlier), and as long as there is no court order to limit your involvement. This means that you are entitled, if you wish, to receive reports on your child, meet or speak to teachers, attend school functions and vote in ballots or elections. You should, however, be sensitive to how your actions will affect your child.

# Age limits for various activities

The law says that young people must reach a certain age before they can do the following activities:

**age 12** • buy a pet

**age 13** • do a part-time job (see Chapter 7 and Appendix 7 for details)

**age 16** • hold a licence for a moped or motorbike under 50cc
• buy and smoke cigarettes
• buy fireworks
• a girl can have sexual intercourse
• change your name with parental consent
• leave home with parental consent
• get married with parental consent
• apply for a passport with parental consent

**age 17** • hold a driving licence for a car or motorbike

**age 18** • get married
• open a bank account
• apply for a passport
• vote in an election

- get a tattoo
- buy and consume alcohol in public
- a man is legally allowed to have a homosexual relationship

**age 21** • stand for election

There are no laws limiting the age for baby-sitting, but someone under 16 is not classed as an adult. Therefore it is the parents of the child who must take responsibility if anything happens to their child whilst in the care of a person under 16 years old.

# Part-time work limits

As indicated in Chapter 7, the restrictions on children doing part-time work are largely governed by local bye-laws. The table below gives one Local Authority's time limits as an example, but you will need to find out from your local Education Office about restrictions that apply in your area.

**EXAMPLE**

| At 13 a child can work on | during the following hours: |
| --- | --- |
| Schooldays | up to two hours a day between 7am and 8.30am in the morning and between the close of school and 7pm in the evening |
| Saturdays | up to five hours, between 7am and 7pm |
| Sundays | up to two hours, between 7am and 11am |
| School holidays | up to five hours a day (except Sundays) between 7am and 7pm, with a *maximum of 25 hours* during one week |

**At 15 a child can work on: during the following hours:**

| | |
|---|---|
| Schooldays | up to two hours a day, between 7am and 8.30 am in the morning, and between the close of school and 7pm in the evening |
| Saturdays | eight hours a day between 7am and 7pm |
| Sundays | up to two hours between 7am and 11am |
| School holidays | up to eight hours a day (except Sundays) between 7am and 7pm, with a *maximum of 35 hours* during one week |

# Curriculum Complaints Procedure

The following procedure for dealing with complaints about curriculum matters, including Religious Education and Worship, was laid down by the Education Reform Act 1988.

The kinds of complaint which should fall under this procedure include ones about:

- National Curriculum and other curriculum matters
- Religious Education and Worship
- withdrawal of your child from the National Curriculum
- the operation of charging policies in relation to the curriculum
- the provision of information to which you are entitled.

The procedure does not cover complaints about admissions or discipline, or the actions of individual members of staff.

The procedure has three distinct stages:

**1 Informal stage**. This will involve discussion between parent and teacher/Headteacher. Most complaints should be resolved at this stage. If not . . .

**2 Formal complaint to the governing body** of the school. If not resolved here then . . .

**3 Formal complaint to the Local Education Authority**. Your complaint can go directly to this stage if it relates to something which is solely the LEA's responsibility.

If your complaint is about Religious Education or Worship and it has not been resolved at stage 2, the LEA may arrange for it to be considered by the local Standing Advisory Council for Religious Education, so that the LEA Complaints Panel at stage 3 has appropriate information and advice.

If your child attends an Aided school and your complaint is about Religious Education or Worship, and it has not been resolved at stage 2, it should then be considered by the Diocesan Authority.

You should be kept informed of progress during as well as at the end of this process. You are entitled to make representations in person at each stage if you wish.

The school or your LEA should advise you on the process. Most LEAs will have a Named Officer for Curriculum Complaints whom you can contact.

If your complaint is not dealt with to your satisfaction by going through the stages described above you can write to the Secretary of State for Education and Employment, whose Department would take it up with the LEA.

# Drugs check-list

The naming of drugs in popular language changes rapidly so if you are to know what your children are talking about, this glossary will give you a start.

| Substance | Slang or brand names |
| --- | --- |
| amphetamines | speed, uppers, whizz, billy, sulphate |
| anabolic steroids | — |
| barbiturates | barbs, blues, downers, reds, sekkies |
| cannabis | dope, grass, hash, shit, blow, wacky baccy, weed |
| cocaine | coke, charlie, snow |
| crack | rock, wash, stone |
| ecstacy | E, disco burgers, New Yorkers, Adam, XTC, fantasy, doves, diamond, rhubarb and custard |
| GHB | GHB (gammahydroxybutyrate), liquid X |
| heroin | smack, junk, H, skag, brown, horse |
| LSD | acid, trips, tab, blotters, dots |
| magic mushrooms | — |
| poppers | (alkyl nitrites) e.g. Liquid Gold, Hi-Tech, Rave |
| Solvents | (such as glues, aerosol sprays, nail varnish remover, butane gas, paint, petrol, dry cleaning fluids) |
| Tranquillisers | e.g. Valium, Temazepam, Librium, Ativan |

# Glossary of acronyms and educational terms

| | |
|---|---|
| ACE | Advisory Centre for Education. Provides advice to parents on education and school issues and publishes a range of helpful ACE Guides. |
| AGIT | Action for Governor Information and Training. A national organisation which provides advice and information for Governors. |
| Aided School | A voluntary school maintained by the LEA in partnership with a religious or charitable body. |
| Ancillary Assistant | A non-teaching member of staff who often supports the work of classroom teachers. |
| Annual Report to Parents | A report on the Governors' work in the preceding year which the governing body is legally required to produce for discussion at the Annual Parents Meeting. |
| AS level | Advanced Subsidiary examination (from 1998). Equivalent in difficulty to A level but covering less content. |
| Assisted Places Scheme | Nationally administered scheme |

|  | providing financial assistance to families to enable children to attend Independent schools. |
| --- | --- |
| Attainment Targets | A National Curriculum term denoting the knowledge, skills and understanding which pupils are expected to acquire by the end of each Key Stage i.e. at 7, 11, 14 and 16. |
| Banding | The grouping of pupils into broad ranges of ability. (Also see Streaming and Setting.) |
| BTEC | Business and Technology Education Council. A body awarding Post-16 vocational qualifications. |
| Capitation | The sum of money within a school's budget allocated for spending on everyday teaching items such as text-books, exercise books, paper, equipment, materials. |
| Catchment area | A defined geographical area from which a school draws most of its pupils. |
| CDT | Craft Design and Technology. |
| City and Guilds | Post-16 vocational qualification awarding body. |
| City Technology College | A state school, independent of the LEA, which provides a curriculum which emphasises Science and Technology. |
| Comprehensive school | Non-selective school (usually refers to secondary) which admits children of all abilities. |
| Controlled school | A voluntary school maintained by the LEA in partnership with a religious or charitable body. |
| Core curriculum | That part of the National Curriculum which must be followed by all pupils of statutory age. |
| Core subjects | English, Mathematics and Science, as identified by the Education Reform Act 1988. |

| | |
|---|---|
| CRE | Commission for Racial Equality. |
| CSE | Certificate of Secondary Education – replaced since 1988 by GCSEs. |
| Curriculum | The learning experiences which are presented to students through lessons and subjects and also through the informal activities and practices of the school. |
| DfEE | Department for Education and Employment (formerly the DES or the DFE). The department of central government responsible for the education service. |
| DT | Design and Technology. |
| Dyslexia | A specific learning difficulty affecting reading and writing development. |
| Education Otherwise | The education of children by their parents or others at home, as a full-time alternative to schooling. |
| Educational Psychologist | A psychologist with a teaching background who assesses pupils and provides advice to schools on special educational needs. |
| EIU | Economic and Industrial Understanding – a cross-curricular aspect of the school curriculum. |
| EWO | Education Welfare Officer. |
| Exclusion | Expulsion from a school on a temporary or permanent basis. |
| FE | Further Education, usually post-16. |
| FEFC | Further Education Funding Council. The body that funds and monitors FE provision. |
| GCSE | General Certificate of Secondary Education. The examination at 16 which replaced O Levels and CSEs in 1988. |
| GNVQ | General National Vocational Qualification. |
| GMS | Grant Maintained Status. When the parents of a school have voted to leave |

the local education authority and be funded directly by the Government.

Governing Body — The group of people who are elected or appointed by the parents, teachers, local education authority, diocese, parish or district council, or co-opted by all of these, to have oversight and give direction to the development of the school.

HE — Higher Education.

HMI — Her Majesty's Inspectorate of schools, now part of the Office for Standards in Education (OFSTED).

Humanities — Those subjects with a social, human or political theme such as Geography, Sociology, and History.

IEP — Individual Education Plan for a child with special educational needs.

In loco parentis — The legal term defining the responsibility teachers have for pupils in their care, (literally means 'in place of a parent').

INSET — In-Service Education and Training for school staff.

IT — Information Technology, such as computers, fax machines, the internet.

Key Stage — Refers to periods of time in the academic life of a pupil: Key Stage 1 is Years 1 and 2; Key Stage 2 is Years 3 to 6; Key Stage 3 is Years 7 to 9; Key Stage 4 is Years 10 and 11, which is the end of compulsory schooling.

LEA — Local Education Authority. That part of the local county, metropolitan or borough council with responsibility for statutory education in its area.

LMS — Local Management of Schools. The scheme whereby schools manage their own budgets and personnel.

LSA — Learning Support Assistant. A non-teaching assistant for pupils with special needs.

HELP YOUR CHILD THROUGH SECONDARY SCHOOL

| | |
|---|---|
| Maintained schools | Schools maintained by the LEA, including County, Controlled and Aided schools (but not Grant Maintained or Independent schools). |
| NCPTA | National Confederation of Parent-Teacher Associations. |
| NAGM | National Association of Governors and Managers (see Chapter 6 for address). |
| NVQ | National Vocational Qualification. |
| NQT | Newly Qualified Teacher in his/her first year of teaching. |
| OFSTED | Office for Standards in Education. Conducts an inspection in every school on a six-yearly basis, or more frequently if needed. |
| OU | Open University. |
| Performance tables | Published results of public examinations and National Tests by school and LEA. |
| Programmes of Study | The content of the teaching programmes laid down within the National Curriculum. |
| Prospectus | An information document about the school which Governors are legally required to publish for parents. |
| PRU | Pupil Referral Unit: provides education for children who are out of school. |
| PSE or PSHE | Personal, Social and Health Education. An element of the curriculum which promotes these aspects of the pupils' development. |
| PTA or PTFA | Parent Teacher Association, Parent, Teachers and Friends Association. |
| RoA | Records of Achievement. |
| SATs | Standard Assessment Tasks, used to ascertain pupils' achievement in the National Curriculum at the end of Key Stages 1, 2 and 3. |
| Setting | Grouping pupils by ability in separate teaching subjects. |
| SEN | Special Educational Needs. |

| | |
|---|---|
| SENCO | Special Educational Needs Co-ordinator within a school. |
| Statement | A Statement of special educational needs describes the special needs of the child and the provision which the school or LEA must make to help the child. |
| Streaming | Grouping pupils by ability for all or most of the subjects in the curriculum. |
| TEC | Training and Enterprise Councils. These are employer-led councils set up by the government to make training and enterprise activities more relevant to employers and individuals at a local level. |
| UCAS | Universities and Colleges Admissions Service. |
| Voluntary school | A group of schools whose history puts them into a slightly different category. They are state schools and receive revenue funding in the same way as LEA maintained schools. Voluntary Aided schools mainly belong to churches or other religious groups or foundations and have to provide and maintain the buildings. The foundation nominates a majority of the governing body, who employ the staff. Voluntary controlled schools usually have a long-standing foundation, not necessarily religious, and the foundation nominates some of the Governors. The school buildings in this case are owned by the Governors but fully maintained by the LEA who also are the staff's employers. |
| Year Group | All the pupils in one year's intake. In secondary schools they are described as Year 7 to Year 13. |

# A reading list for Key Stage 3 boys (aged 11 to 14)

It is widely recognised that boys lose interest in reading in the 11 to 14 age range and it is felt that this hinders their progress in English and in other subjects. The Kirklees Education Advisory Service has produced a pack for teachers on *Raising Boys' Achievement* which includes the following reading list – reproduced here with permission. Readers interested in obtaining further details from Kirklees should ring 01484 225793.

**Blackman, Marjorie,** *Hacker,* Corgi (1994). ISBN: 0 552 52751 3
**Bradman, Tony,** (Collected by), *Amazing adventure stories,* Corgi (1995). ISBN: 0 552 52768 8
**Bradman, Tony,** (Collected by), *Fantastic space stories,* Corgi (1995). ISBN: 0 552 52767 X
**Buchan, John,** *The thirty-nine steps,* Dent (1992).
ISBN: 0 460 88128 0
**Burgess, Melvin,** *The cry of the wolf,* Puffin (1992).
ISBN: 014 037318 7
**Burgess, Melvin,** *The baby and Fly Pie,* Andersen (1993).
ISBN: 0 86264 461 5
**Blacker, Terence,** *Homebird,* Piper (1992). ISBN: 0330 31998 1

**Corlett, William,** *The steps up the chimney,* Red Fox (1991).
ISBN: 0 09 985370 1
**Deery, Terry,** *The Horrible History Series,* Hippo (Scholastic).
**Fine, Anne,** *Flour Babies,* Puffin (1994). ISBN: 0 14 036147 2
**Gleeson, Libby,** *Dodger,* Puffin (1992). ISBN: 0 14 036063 8
**Gleitzman, Morris,** *Two weeks with the Queen,* Piper (1990).
ISBN: 0 330 31376 2
**Goscinny,** *Asterix series,* Hodder.
**Herge,** *Tintin series,* Methuen.
**Horowitz, Anthony,** *Groosham Grange,* Walker Books (1994).
ISBN: 0 7 445 2476 8
**Horowitz, Anthony (Ed.),** *The Puffin book of horror stories,* Puffin
(1994). ISBN: 0 14 036883 3
**Jacques, Brian,** *Redwall,* Red Fox (1989). ISBN: 0 09 951200 9
**Jacques, Brian,** *Salamandastron,* Red Fox (1994). ISBN:
0 09 914361 5
**Jarvis, Robin,** *The Whitby Witches,* Simon and Schuster Young
Books (1991). ISBN: 0 7500 1581 5
**Jarvis, Robin,** *The warlock in Whitby,* Simon and Schuster Young
Books (1991). ISBN: 0 7500 1203 X
**Jarvis, Robin,** *The Deptford Mice trilogy,* Macdonald Young Books
(1996). ISBN: 0 7500 2201 9
**Jarvis, Robin,** *The woven path,* Collins (1995).
ISBN: 0 00 675012 5
**Jennings, Paul,** *Unbearable!* Puffin (1991). ISBN: 0 14 037103 6
**Jennings, Paul,** *Unmentionable!* Puffin (1991). ISBN: 0 14 037104 4
**Jennings, Paul,** *Unreal!* Puffin (1991). ISBN: 0 14 037099 4
**Jordan, Sherryl,** *Rocco,* Andre Deutsch (1992).
ISBN: 0 590 54005 X
**Kilworth, Garry,** *The drowners,* Mammoth (1992).
ISBN: 0 7497 1049 7
**Kilworth, Garry,** *The electric kid,* Bantam Books (1995).
ISBN: 0 553 40656 6
**Laird, Elizabeth,** *Kiss the dust,* Mammoth (1991).
ISBN: 0 7497 0857 3

**Leonard, Alison,** *Kiss the Kremlin goodbye,* Walker Books (1991). ISBN: 0 7445 2360 5

**Pettit, Jayne,** *A time to fight back,* Macmillan (1995). ISBN: 0330 34133 2

**Pettit, Jayne,** *A place to hide,* Piper (1995). ISBN: 0 330 33883 5

**Pope, James,** *Magnificent!,* Red Fox (1993). ISBN: 0 09 914181 7

**Porritt, Jonathon and Nadler, Ellis,** *Captain Eco and the fate of the Earth,* Dorling Kindersley (1991). ISBN: 9 780863 187032

**Pratchett, Terry,** *Only you can save mankind,* Corgi (1993). ISBN: 0 552 13926 2

**Pratchett, Terry,** *Johnny and the dead,* Corgi (1994). ISBN: 0 552 52740 8

**Pratchett, Terry,** *Johnny and the bomb,* Doubleday (1996). ISBN: 0 385 40670 3

**Pratchett, Terry,** *Truckers,* Corgi (1990). ISBN: 0 552 52595 2

**Pratchett, Terry,** *Diggers,* Corgi (1990). ISBN: 0 552 52585 3

**Pratchett, Terry,** *Wings,* Corgi (1990). ISBN: 0 552 52649 5

**Pullman, Philip,** *Count Karlstein,* Corgi (1991). ISBN: 0 440 86266 3

**Pullman, Philip,** *Spring-heeled Jack,* Corgi (1991). ISBN: 0 440 86229 9

**Pullman, Philip,** *Thunderbolt's waxwork,* Puffin (1996). ISBN: 0 14 036410 2

**Ridley, Philip,** *Krindlekrax,* Red Fox (1992). ISBN: 0 09 997920 9

**Ridley, Philip,** *Kaspar in the glitter,* Puffin (1992). ISBN: 0 14 026891 4

**Ridley, Philip,** *Meteorite spoon,* Puffin (1992). ISBN: 0 14 036890

**Swindells, Robert,** *Inside the worm,* Yearling (1994). ISBN: 0 440 86300 7

**Swindells, Robert,** *Brother in the land,* Puffin (1994). ISBN: 0 14 037300 4

**Swindells, Robert,** *Room 13,* Yearling (1994). ISBN: 0 440 86227 2

**Swindells, Robert,** *Daz 4 Zoe,* Puffin (1995). ISBN: 0 14 037264 4

**Taylor, Clark,** *The house that Crack built.* Chronicle Books (1994).

(Available from Letterbox Library, tel: 0171 226 1633. Code no. for the book is 4444.) ISBN: 0 8118 0123 3

**Westall, Robert,** *The kingdom by the sea,* Mammoth (1992). ISBN: 0 7497 0796 8

**Westall, Robert,** *Yaxley's cat,* Piper (1992). ISBN: 0 333 32499 3

**Westall, Robert,** *The stones of Muncaster Cathedral,* Puffin (1992). ISBN: 0 14 037358 6

**Westall, Robert,** *A time of fire,* Piper (1995). ISBN: 0 330 33754 8

**Westall, Robert,** *The machine gunners,* Piper (1995). ISBN: 0 330 33428 X

**Westall, Robert,** *Blitzcat,* Piper (1990). ISBN: 0 330 31040 2

**Westall, Robert,** *Gulf,* Mammoth (1993). ISBN: 0 7497 1472 7

**Westwood, Chris,** *Brother of mine,* Puffin (1994). ISBN: 0 14 037828 6

**Woodford, Peggy,** *Blood and mortar,* Corgi Freeway (1994). ISBN: 0 552 52774 2

(A fuller list with prices and synopses of stories can be obtained from Young Book Trust. See list of useful addresses.)

# Additional useful addresses

Most addresses are listed at the end of the relevant chapter.

## *Education Departments*

**Department for Education and Employment (DfEE),** Sanctuary Buildings, Great Smith Street, London SW1P 3BT. Tel: 0171 925 6474.

**DfEE Publications Department,** PO Box 2193, London E15 2EU. Tel: 0181 533 2000.

**Northern Ireland Department of Education,** Rathgael House, Balloo Road, Bangor, Co. Down BT19 7PR. Tel: 01247 270077.

**Welsh Office Education Department,** Government Buildings, Ty Glas Road, Llanishen, Cardiff CF4 5WE. Tel: 01222 825111.

**Scottish Office Education Department,** New St. Andrew's House, Edinburgh EH1 3TD. Tel: 0131 244 4445.

# General information

**The Advisory Centre for Education** is an independent national advisory service offering free advice, information and support to parents and pupils in state schools. It has a wide range of booklets and information sheets. Write to ACE, 1b Aberdeen Studios, 22-24 Highbury Grove, London N5 2DQ. For publications phone 0171 354 8321 and for advice phone 0171 354 8321, between 2 and 5 pm.

**Careers Research Advisory Council (CRAC),** 2nd Floor, Sheraton House, Castle Park, Cambridge CB3 0AX. Tel: 01223 460277.

**Her Majesty's Stationery Office (HMSO),** Publications Centre, PO Box 276, London SW8 5DT. Tel: 0171 873 9090. HMSO publishes Education Acts and other policy and guidance documents which may be of interest.

**Local Government Ombudsman** There are three Regional Offices: 21 Queen Anne's Gate, London SW1H 9BU. Tel: 0171 915 3210. This covers Greater London, Kent, East and West Sussex, and Surrey.
The Oaks, 2 Westwood Way, Westwood Business Park, Coventry CV4 8JB. Tel: 01203 695999. This covers East Anglia, the South West, South and Central England.
Beverley House, 17 Shipton Road, York YO3 6FZ. Tel: 01904 663200. This covers Cheshire, Derbyshire, Nottinghamshire, Lincolnshire and the North of England.

**Young Book Trust,** Book House, 45 East Hill, London SW18 2QZ. Tel: 01853 534578.

# Index

# Positive Parenting

**Positive parenting** is a series of handbooks primarily written for parents, in a clear, accessible style, giving practical information, sound advice and sources of specialist and general help. Based on the authors' extensive professional and personal experience, they cover a wide range of topics and provide an invaluable source of encouragement and information to all who are involved in child care in the home and in the community.

Other books in this series include:

**Talking and your child 0 340 57526 3** by Clare Shaw – a guide outlining the details of how speech and language develops from birth to age 11 and how parents can help with the process.

**Your child from 5–11 0 340 54750 2** by Jennie and Lance Lindon – a guide showing parents how they can help their children through these crucial early years, stressing the contribution a caring family can make to the emotional, physical and intellectual development of the child.

**Help your child through school 0 340 60796 3** by Jennie and Lance Lindon – a guide which looks at the school years from the perspective of the family, showing how parents can help their children to get the most out of their years at primary school and how to ease the transition into secondary education.

**Help your child with maths 0 340 60767 X** by Sue Atkinson – a comprehensive guide to show parents how they can help develop their children's mathematical awareness and confidence from babyhood through the primary years and into secondary school.

**Help your child with reading and writing 0 340 60768 8** by Lesley Clark – a guide which describes the stages children go through when learning to read and write and shows parents how they can encourage and enjoy their children's early development in these vital areas.

**Prepare your child for school 0 340 60797 1** by Clare Shaw – a very practical guide for parents whose children are about to start school.

HELP YOUR CHILD THROUGH SECONDARY SCHOOL

**Help your child with a foreign language 0 340 60766 1** by Opal Dunn – written for all parents, including those who do not speak a foreign language, this guide examines the right time to start teaching a child a foreign language, how to begin, and how to progress to fluency.

**Teenagers in the family 0 340 62106 0** by Debi Roker and John Coleman of the Trust for Adolescence covers all the major issues that parents face as their children pass through the turbulent teenage years, such as rules and regulations, setting boundaries, communication, decision making, risky behaviour, health issues, and problems at school.

**Teenagers and sexuality 0 340 62105 2** by John Coleman of the Trust for Adolescence gives practical advice for parents who are finding it difficult to talk to their teenagers about sex and who need help to understand, and deal with, their teenagers' emerging sexuality.

**Help your child with homework and exams 0 340 65866 5** by Jennie Lindon offers parents practical advice on how they can help their children to take a positive approach to homework and exams across the whole school curriculum.

**Help your child be confident 0 340 67004 5** by Clare Shaw is packed full of ideas for parents on how to build their children's confidence, ensuring that children grow up feeling good about themselves and the world around them.

**Help your child through the National Curriculum 0 340 66936 5** by Graeme Kent is a practical guide that shows how parents can help their primary school child cope with and enjoy the subjects of the National Curriculum and prepare for Key Stage 1 and 2 Assessment Tests.